Cynthia Boris Liljeblad

Published by

**krause
publications**

700 E. State Street • Iola, WI 54990-0001
Telephone: 715/445-2214

Please call or write for our free catalog of Toys & Comics publications.
Our toll-free number to place an order or obtain a free catalog is 800-258-0929 or please use our regular business
telephone 715-445-2214 for editorial comment and further information.

Library of Congress Catalog Number: 95-82426
ISBN: 0-87341-440-3
Printed in the United States of America

A special thanks to photographer Mary Platt, and Sharon Korbeck,
editor of *Toy Shop*, for providing photos for this book.

DEDICATION

This book is dedicated to all the dealers, collectors, and manufacturers. Without them there would be nothing to write about. This book is also for Kathy Clark, who is not a writer, a photographer, or any of the above, but she suffered the labor pains of its birth as I did. Thanks for the ear and the push.

ACKNOWLEDGMENTS

Additional thanks to :

Joshua and Lars Liljeblad
Jeanne Gold
The crew at TBP, Santa Ana
Deborah Faupel of Krause Publications for believing it would work, and
Mary Platt for putting up with me while she took pictures!

CONTENTS

INTRODUCTION

If you were a child of the sixties, chances are you watched *Lost in Space*, or *Bonanza*, or *The Rat Patrol* with astonishing regularity. I'd also bet you spent a good portion of your play time pretending to be a character from that favorite series. And why not? What little boy wouldn't want to be Will Robinson or Zorro, and how many little girls envisioned themselves as a nurse to Dr. Kildare or the very first girl from U.N.C.L.E.? That's what TV toys were all about. They were designed to make kids feel like a part of their favorite television series.

Let's go back to that era for just a moment. Back then, the toy business was completely different from the way it is today. There was no Toys R Us, no Kay-bee, just Mr. and Mrs. Grabowski who ran the five-and-dime on the corner. Where I came from, we called those variety stores. You know the kind—where Mom could buy a needle and thread to fix a hem and I could buy a new toy. In the fifties, kids would run into the store with their five-cent allowance and buy whatever attracted their fancy. The sixties and the advent of television changed all that. Toy companies soon realized that a hit TV series was as good as a multi-million dollar ad campaign with no money out of pocket. So began the phenomenon of TV licensing. Companies were creating a market for their toys and salesmen were hitting the road with cases full of TV tie-in products. A plastic horse might sell for ten cents, but a plastic horse with the official *Bonanza* logo attached to it could sell for fifty cents. These toys would literally sell themselves and any toy store caught without—well sorry, that generic toy horse just wouldn't do (even though it was probably made by the same company as the licensed one). Suddenly kids were going into the dime store and asking for products by name and company. "I want Little Joe's Palomino by American Character." If you think that's an exaggeration, think again. Toy companies wanted to be sure their licensed product, not a bootleg version, was being bought. They created catch phrases and commercials that directed buyers right to their product. Remember "You can tell it's Mattel--It's Swell!!" and "It's a Wonderful Toy--It's Ideal!" Toy companies were selling packaging. A recognizable box with a well-known face made even the most common toys something special. Generic army jeeps became The Rat Patrol Play Set! A toy dashboard turned into the pilot's console from *Land of the Giants*!

The toy companies that gave us so much pleasure back then have all but vanished, with Mattel being the only survivor thanks to a real doll named Barbie. The company was named after its two founders, Matson and Elliott, but it was an electronics engineer named Jack Ryan that gave Mattel its edge. Ryan was the developer of Mattel's pull-string talk box and soon every creature in their line, from The Monkees to Herman Munster, could talk. It was a technique that would not be improved upon until the invention of microchip technology.

Leading the pack since the early 1900s was the Louis Marx Company, famous for their detailed play sets. Marx moved into the sixties with a marketing plan that didn't include the mom-and-pop stores. They sold exclusives to large chain stores like Sears and Montgomery Ward. These special issues, which were generally made for the Christmas catalogs, are some of the most sought after collectibles in the biz. By 1972, a time when many food companies were buying toy companies, Marx sold the business to Quaker Oats, but Quaker never managed to maintain its success. They gave up the toy line a few years later.

Transogram was another holdover from the early 1900s. Their games and plastic play sets were marketed in discount stores like Grant's, but the company was sold in the seventies and soon disbanded.

When it came to coloring books and paper dolls, Whitman (also known as Western Publishing) and Saalfield were kings in the sixties. The Saalfield family had been around since the thirties, with the license to Shirley Temple being their key money-maker. In the seventies, Rand McNally bought the publishing house and gave up the name. Whitman has held on, returning to its original name of Western Publishing, and is responsible for most of the TV coloring books, paper dolls and puzzles of the sixties. Don't forget those famous chunky Whitman TV novels for young readers.

Ideal has also been around since the early 1900s. The company's founder, Morris Michtom, dove into the toy business when he saw a cartoon of then president Teddy Roosevelt refusing to shoot a bear cub during a hunting trip. Michtom asked the president if he could use his name on a stuffed bear he was planning to produce. Roosevelt doubted that his name would carry much weight, but said O.K. The rest is history. Actually, Ideal became the main source of upper level dolls, including Patti Playpal and the Toni dolls, but don't think they were all hits. In 1957, Ben Michtom created the Baby Jesus doll, a concept that nearly bankrupted the company. (Just how does one mark down Jesus Christ?) In the 1980s Ideal was bought by CBS with hopes of capturing the new electronic toy market. Their hopes were never realized, so the company was broken up, the molds and patents sold off to other toy companies. As a whole, the Ideal Toy and Novelty Company became another casualty of the modern age.

And now, I've saved my favorites for last. The Aurora Plastics Company was on the receiving end of more than half of my allowances as a kid. Aurora started making models in 1952. Like most companies of the day, they started out with airplanes and military vehicles. Then in the early sixties they switched their focus to figures and offered a contest asking people to submit ideas for their new line. A young boy suggested monsters and a hit was born. Aurora became king of the model business in the sixties with their highly detailed versions of Dracula, Frankenstein and the Wolfman, so it was only natural that they jump on the TV bandwagon with kits based on Batman, Zorro and the men from U.N.C.L.E. One of the keys to Aurora's success was the effort that went into creating the box art for their kits. Artists were commissioned to design and paint elaborate canvases that were then sized down to fit the box. It is this attention to detail that makes Aurora models the high ticket items that they are. And if you think a kit is expensive, try getting your hands on some of that Aurora original art-work—it's worth thousands. Unfortunately, Aurora also fell victim to the conglomerate buying craze of the seventies. The company was purchased by Nabisco, the family cookie king. Within days of the announcement, Nabisco execs were horrified to find a line of demonstrators outside their offices protesting the gruesome monster kits that had made Aurora its money. The cookie company quickly issued a press release saying they would cease production of the more violent kits while toning down the creepy kits with a comic twist. It was the death toll for Aurora. Nabisco was forced to break up the company and sell it less than five years after its acquisition. Here the rumors kick in.

Most of the model molds were sold to and reissued by Monogram in later years (some are still being released today), but there is a story about many of the original molds being destroyed in a train wreck.

Last and best on my list is the often maligned but never topped Remco. Remco was the baby of the group, forming in 1949 and ceasing production in 1970, a short run compared to its competition. In the mid-sixties Remco was on fire thanks to two inventions: plastic and the battery. Think about the early life of mass-produced toys. They were generally made of metal, and if they moved it was thanks to bulky keys stuck in their sides. When the world moved into the space age, Remco went right along inventing toys that walked and moved, blinked and beeped, thanks to the wonder of a battery pack. And talk about big!! If you see a toy in a huge box, it's probably a Remco toy. Actually, it's a wonder they went out of business considering their penchant for recycling. It would appear the company made only about fifty different toys, they just kept repackaging them. Design a new box, add a photo of the cast, slap on a logo sticker, and you've got a hot seller. Show goes off the air, trash the box, peel off the sticker, you're back in business again. Remco's plastic flying helicopter became the Batman Copter. Their miniature military jeep became The Rat Patrol Midget Motors Jeep. Worst of all, there's a bazooka/Tommy gun/Torpedo gun that became the Voyage to the Bottom of the Sea Sub Gun, a toy that didn't resemble anything you would ever see on the show. My hat goes off to the ingenuity of Remco.

Of course, that isn't all. Milton Bradley, Parker Bros., Topps, Aladdin, MPC, Revell, GAF and Colorforms—there isn't a toy company in the U.S. that didn't play the licensing game at one time. But no matter which toy you are seeking or which company made it, you can be sure of two things: You'll never buy it for the price you paid in 1966, and nothing will ever be worth more than owning a toy your mom threw away when you were a kid. In my old neighborhood, some trashman is makin' himself a bundle of dough.

Tips for Collectors

Condition

Most items in stores and catalogs are graded with some variation of poor, fair, good, near mint and mint. Unfortunately, condition is generally in the eye of the beholder, and one person's "fair" is another's "poor." When it comes to toys of the sixties there really are only two options: played with and not played with. A toy that has never been played with obviously commands a higher price. Toys that show signs of childhood abuse can go for less than half the market rate. Here are a few things to look for when deciding price based on condition.

Mint in box should mean still in its original box, oftentimes still shrink-wrapped, with no signs of water damage or tears in the box. The box may be slightly dull in color since it is difficult to stop dust from settling in the cardboard fibers. The toy itself should look like new—no cracks, no tears, no missing pieces. If it did something in 1968, it should still do it now, i.e. walk or talk. Model prices are based on being unassembled with parts still on the part trees, those silly plastic pieces that you never knew what to do with. The instructions should still be in the box.

If a toy does not meet the above qualifications, it's not mint. Don't pay top dollar unless you can't live without it. Most toys are still considered collectible even with minor damage. Near mint, good, and fair are all ways of saying that a toy has been touched by a kid or kids. The box may be gone, the battery compartment may be rusted, and the plastic may have hairline cracks. Warping and water damage are common in boxes from the era, but if the damage is in a small hidden spot like the bottom flap, go for it.

When it comes to poor condition, it's a judgment call for the buyer. Some people have to own every toy ever made for a show even if it's worthless on a resale market. That's cool as long as you know what you're doing. That rusted *Lost in Space* lunch box with stickers all over the back and Joey Hinton's name written across the face in permanent marker will never make it to the head of Toy Scouts' auction block. But if it's cheap and you really want a *Lost in Space* lunch box, even a trashed one, then buy it. Collecting is often about trading up as you find better versions of things you own.

Prices

Let's all repeat this: "A GOOD PRICE IS THE PRICE YOU'RE WILLING TO PAY FOR AN ITEM!" Did everybody get that? Make it your mantra when you go to a toy show. I don't care if this book and six others quote a *Rat Patrol* Diorama at $100. If the dealer is selling it for $150 and you can afford to pay $150, then it's a good, fair price. Buy it. The sentence we want to eliminate from your vocabulary is, "I should have bought it when I saw it." Price guides are called GUIDES for a reason. They are just that, guides, not prices set in stone, not binding, not legal. This is especially true if you're trying to sell your collection. A *Lost in Space* Roto Jet gun once sold for $14,000 at auction. Now hold on, don't put the money down on that boat yet. If the average guy sells a Roto Jet gun to a dealer he'll probably get $150 to $200 for it. If he advertises and sells to a collector he might make $500 or more; rarely will he make top dollar. Why? Markets are fickle and dealers need to make a profit. For every Roto Jet gun, they have ninety-five *Welcome Back, Kotter* coloring books and sixty-four *Charlie's Angels* make-up kits. Thus the phrase, "it's okay, you'll make it up in volume." Dealers have to sell dozens of toys for a wide range of prices just to break even every month, so they have to buy their stock at less than half the going price. Yes, I said half. When it comes to selling to a dealer, consider yourself blessed if you get half the going rate.

Here's a tip: trade. Easy, huh? You were into *Batman* three years ago; now you're into *The Addams Family* (the release of major movies will do that to you). Suggest a trade—your Corgi Batmobile for a set of Addams Family puppets. You swap and everybody goes home with something fresh. You just never know what a dealer will trade for until you ask. He may have two guys willing to pay $2,000 for that Corgi Batmobile. Remember the mantra. Say it again: **"A Good Price is what you're willing to pay for an item."** Good. The second part: never look back. Once you've made a deal, it's history. There's no sense making yourself crazy with, "I could have got it for less" or "sold it for more." Are you pleased with your find? Then take it and run. That's the only way to collect.

One last tip: True fans of a TV show collect for that warm fuzzy feeling the toy evokes in them. A nice resale price is just a bonus. For most collectors, the items will stay on their shelves and in their hearts until the day they die. Then only their heirs will learn how valuable this stuff really is.

Now having said all that, read this book, highlight items, fold down corners, USE IT. Carry it with you to a toy show, make it your friend and keep repeating that mantra. Yes, you've got it: "A good price is the price you're willing to pay for an item." Hit the cash machine before you go in (only a small portion of dealers take credit cards) and give yourself a budget. Now go, shop, have fun, say ooh and aah, and tell everybody, "I had that when I was a kid." Dealers hate when you say that, it's really fun. When you spot that *Lost in Space* Robot with the logo stickers torn off and a crack in the bubble, with no box for $700—the book says pay no more than $400, you budgeted $500—plunk down your money, scoop up your prize and start imagining how it will look on your mantle. As you walk away with that warm fuzzy feeling eating you up inside, revel in the sound of all those other collectors whispering, "Wow, look what he got. Aw man, I've been looking for one of those forever. I wonder if he got a good deal?"

Throughout the book you'll find this little piggy bank symbol next to some items. This is my "Worth It at Any Price" designation. No matter what you specialize in— Westerns, Sci-fi, character dolls, lunch boxes—there are certain toys that you just must have. Sometimes it's because they're just downright fun; sometimes it's because they're overwhelmingly tacky. Either way, my piggy bank items are worth every dime. Just spot one and see if you don't agree.

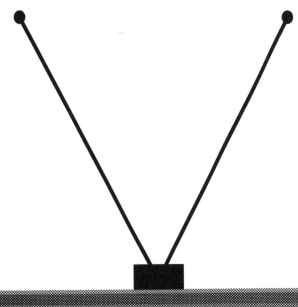

LAUGHING ALL THE WAY TO THE BANK:

COMEDY ON TELEVISION

Will Rogers once said, "Everything is funny as long as it is happening to somebody else." Isn't that the truth. Slamming our hand in a piano sounds painful, but when Dick Van Dyke does it, we roll off the couch with laughter. War is a seemingly depressing topic, but Hogan and his heroes were laughing all the way to the bank. And think of three children, orphaned and alone, forced to live with an uncle they've never met. Horrible thought? No, it's *Family Affair*.

Comedy wears many faces. In the early years of television, family life situations were the mainstay of comedy on television. The situation comedy, or sitcom as it is called, was funny because we saw ourselves in the picture. *Make Room for Daddy, The Andy Griffith Show, The Donna Reed Show*—week after week, their plots seemed interchangeable. The male lead has to decide between seeing his kids in a play or leaving town on business. Is it Danny Thomas or Dick Van Dyke? The girls decide to get a job as roller skating waitresses. Could be *The Brady Bunch*, could be *The Patty Duke Show*. Americans didn't care about the simplicity of the plot. They were enchanted with the characters and drawn into lives that resembled their own.

As we moved into the mid-sixties, comedy took a turn toward the weird. A reflection of the times, no doubt. Now the family down the block had a hearse parked in front of the house and a grandfather with a taste for fresh blood. The new little girl in the first grade carried a headless doll and Paul Revere was a frequent visitor on Morning Glory Circle. On *The Munsters, The Addams Family*, and *Bewitched*, magic was equal to merriment. In the age of hippies and draft dodgers, political and social satire came into vogue. Remember *Laugh-In* with President Richard Nixon asking us to "sock it to him?" Even *The Monkees* poked fun at the "Establishment," as four long-haired rock and roll musicians tried to make it in a world that gave preference to clean-cut college boys. Then there was that symbol of government efficiency, Maxwell Smart.

With the approach of the seventies, comedy began to take a look at our fears. Doctors faced death every week on *M*A*S*H*. A single woman tried to survive on her own in *The Mary Tyler Moore Show*, and the ugly face of prejudice was brought into millions of homes in *All in the Family*. In *Good Times, Welcome Back, Kotter*, and *Sanford and Son*, gone were the pristine homes with manicured lawns. The family situations were no longer so simple; now the family was faced with teenage pregnancy, suicide, and gang war.

From its birth to the present, the many faces of comedy have been there to entertain, educate and prompt us to think. We've grown attached to those weekly visits with our TV friends and we care about them. Millions of people witnessed the birth of Little Ricky on *I Love Lucy*, and almost as many tuned in to see Mary Richards leave the newsroom for one last time. When it comes to toys, more character-inspired dolls are found in this genre of television than any other. You can own your very own set of *My Three Sons* twins, or a Buffy doll with a tiny Mrs. Beasley in tow. You can buy a Herman Munster talking puppet or a beautiful *Bewitched* doll complete with witch's broom. With toys like these, it's obvious that when it comes to sitcoms, it's not the props or the places that are important, it's the people.

BEWITCHED

September 1964 - July 1972

Submitted for your approval, one Darrin Stephens, a man who could have everything—power, prestige, cash and cars—but asks nothing except the love of a good woman and a home cooked meal. Darrin Stephens is living in the Bewitched Zone. Loosely based on the movie *I Married a Witch*, the story of *Bewitched* surrounded Samantha Stephens, a lovely witch who could twitch her nose and make anyone's wish come true. Samantha (Elizabeth Montgomery) preferred the life of a mortal once she met and married her true love, Darrin. Darrin was originally played by Dick York, but when York grew ill during the run, he was replaced by Dick Sargent. (Kind of like the two Marilyns on *The Munsters*.) Darrin worked for the advertising agency of McMahon and Tate, giving the writers an out for many of the kooky things that happened. Seventy-five percent of all plot twists were explained away as advertising stunts.

Adding spice to the humdrum mortal life were Samantha's family members who were constantly popping in. Agnes Moorehead is still captivating as Endora, Samantha's mother. Endora was normally seen in a gauzy flowing gown that floated around her while she floated on air (all the better to eavesdrop, my dear). Samantha's father Maurice was played by the Shakespearean actor Maurice Evans. While not quite as flamboyant as his TV wife, Evans always commanded attention on-screen with his distinguished good looks and commanding English voice. Paul Lynde (well-known for his time as a Hollywood Square) made frequent appearances as Sam's Uncle Arthur, an incorrigible practical joker with a fondness for turning Darrin into an animal of some sort. Esmerelda, played by Alice Ghostley, was the witch who tended to fade when things went wrong. Marion Lorne often joined the group as Aunt Clara, the bumbling witch whose spells tended to go haywire although she had the best of intentions. Curing the family's ills was Bernard Fox as the "witch doctor" Bombay. His cures were often worse than the diseases. And lest we forget, there was Samantha's swinging look-alike cousin Serena, played by Montgomery herself in a black wig.

On the side of the mortals, Darrin had a few supporters. David White was excellent as Darrin's boss Larry Tate. Poor Larry was on the receiving end of many bits of magic, but nothing that a stiff drink couldn't put asunder. Beside Larry was his wife Louise, played by the still lovely Kasey Rogers. And who is that lady peering in the kitchen window anyway? It's Gladys Kravitz, the neighborhood busybody that no one will listen to. Actress Alice Pearce was posthumously given an Emmy for her role when she died in 1966. Filling her shoes was Sandra Gould as the wife to the long suffering Abner Kravitz (George Tobias). Two years into the run of the series, the Stephens family grew with the birth of Tabitha. It took three sets of twins to play the baby until two-year-old Erin Murphy assumed the role in the fall of 1966. Tabitha's birth was a much awaited event but the really big question for audiences was, "Will she be a witch or a mortal?" It didn't take long for the baby to exercise her powers, leaving Darrin with a little more explaining to do. In 1969, Adam, the Stephens's second child, was born but rarely seen until the show moved into the seventies.

Even now, some thirty years later, the show remains fresh and easy to watch. Elizabeth Montgomery's everyday housewife image was a nice change from the high-heeled Donna Reed moms of the fifties. The entire cast is enjoyable, the guests delightful, and the plots imaginative. As for the special effects, not even modern technology can do a better job at making dishes fly, people disappear and toys talk, and nobody, I mean nobody, can twitch a nose like Samantha.

Bewitched Collectibles

			Mint	Ex	Good
ACTIVITY BOOK	**Treasure Books**	**1965**	**15**	**8**	**5**

Oddly enough, this book is very common. You see it at almost every toy show, thus the low ticket price. The cover features a nice photo of Samantha, Endora, and Darrin. Inside it's basically an educational coloring book.

BROOM	**Amsco**	**1965**	**50**	**27**	**15**

This little ditty came from a company specializing in playhouse toys (see Magic Coffee set below). The broom was thirty-six inches long and had a plastic Samantha head on top. All ready for sweeping or flying.

COLORING BOOK	**Treasure Books**	**1965**	**30**	**15**	**10**

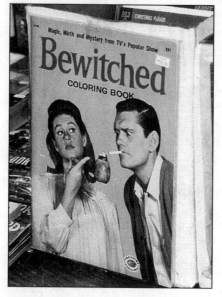

This is a tougher find than the activity book above. Expect to pay more.

DOLL, SAMANTHA	**Ideal**	**1965**	**400**	**220**	**120**

This beautiful doll came in a box with a clear window. She is about the size of a Barbie doll and she came dressed in a sparkling red gown with a matching witch's hat. The doll bears little resemblance to Elizabeth Montgomery, but it is still highly collectible with TV fans and character doll collectors.

			Mint	Ex	Good
FEEDING SET	Amsco	1965	150	82	45

Ah, the Magic Baby Bottle people are at it again. (You remember—the bottle that has milk disappear by magic when your doll drinks it.) This set was labeled "A Travel Bag Full of Magic," but no spells were included, only some plates, spoons, and bottles for feeding your baby. The set was packed in a vinyl bag sporting the series' logo.

GAME, BOARD	T. Cohn	1965	40	22	12

On the cover of this board game is a very cute graphic of Endora and Samantha "in flight" with actual photos of the actresses heads attached to cartoon bodies. (This was undoubtedly easier than photographing both actresses in actual flight.)

GAME, CARD	Milton Bradley	1964	30	17	9

This card game was called Stymie. It came in a 6" x 10" box with a small graphic of the three leads on the left. The game came with a vinyl play board and a deck of cards.

HI-CHAIR SET	Amsco	1965	200	110	60

How many shows can claim their very own hi-chair and feeding set? Not many. The chair came with a plethora of tiny feeding tools. The only thing missing is Tabitha!

MAGIC COFFEE SET	Amsco	1965	125	70	40

As play sets go, this is a real rarity. While cowboy outfits were big in the sixties, this set was made for little girls to play house. It included a coffee pot, toaster, burner, and cups, all with the *Bewitched* logo. The box itself has the logo in very small print (the Amsco advertising department wasn't paying attention at work that day).

PAPER DOLL	Magic Wand	1965	50	27	15

Ask the girls in the group if they remember Magic Wand paper dolls. This invention was kind of a cross between normal paper dolls and colorforms. The doll was made of stiff cardboard and coated with a thin film. The "magic wand" was a plastic stick that created static electricity when you ran it over the doll so the clothes would stick. Very clever until the doll got covered in grime and dust, then forget it. This kit has a nice photo on the cover of Sam at the front door.

THE ADDAMS FAMILY

September 1964 - September 1966

They're creepy and they're kooky, mysterious and spooky, they're all together ooky, (sing it now) The Addams Family. And don't forget the appropriate finger snaps along the way. When composer Vic Mizzy made up those nonsensical rhymes, he had no idea he was writing himself into TV history. But that's getting a bit ahead of the game.

In the 1940s, cartoonist Charles Addams gave birth to the family of oddballs with his single-celled cartoons that made frequent appearances in *The New Yorker* magazine. It was nearly 1964 when the cartoons came to the attention of former TV executive David Levy. Thinking he had found something truly new and different, Levy saw in the bizarre characters the makings of a hit TV show. It is only a strange, and I do mean strange, coincidence that *The Munsters* was gearing up for production at the same time. With the permission of Charles Addams, Levy sold the idea to Filmways, the studio that put *Mr. Ed* and *The Beverly Hillbillies* on the air. John Astin (Gomez Addams) was in on the project from the beginning, except he wasn't slated to play the peculiar patriarch; he was supposed to be Lurch the butler. It took many screen tests and discarded choices before the studio settled on their cast. Astin became Gomez, the overexuberant father figure with a penchant for expensive cigars and pinstripe suits. Carolyn Jones, wife of TV icon Aaron Spelling, donned the black wig and skintight gown to play Morticia. Former child star Jackie Coogan wanted the part of Uncle Fester, but was turned down until he showed up bald, costumed and made-up to resemble the Fester of Addams's cartoons. Ken Weatherwax, nephew of Lassie trainer, Bud, became pudgy little Pugsley, and the role of Wednesday fell to future soap star Lisa Loring when she was still too young to read her own scripts. Grandmama was played by the truly regal and stunning Blossom Rock (yes, that is her real name), big sister of movie legend Jeannette McDonald. And answering the sound of the gong as Lurch was Ted Cassidy, all 6' 9", 250 pounds of him. Now here's a secret, lean closer to the book: It was Ted Cassidy's hand that made regular appearances as Thing, the family's faithful "handyman."

On call for guest appearances was midget actor Felix Silla as Cousin ITT—you remember, the little hairy one with the bowler hat. Here's another secret: ITT's voice was that of sound engineer Tony Magro. If you listen to ITT talk, you'll swear his voice is made of natural speech speeded up, but that is just a testament to Magro's handiwork. Actually, his voice was done by speeding up a tape of gibberish syllables with the inflections adjusted to fit the mood of the scene.

When you think *Addams Family*, think harpsichord music, Cleopatra the man-eating plant, Wednesday's headless doll, and Gomez's trains forever set on a collision course. But here's one more secret: the "group" you hear singing the theme each week is actually just composer Mizzy and his music editor Dave Kahn exercising their vocal chords with a little help from Ted Cassidy. This group excelled at making use of what they had.

Addams Family Collectibles

			Mint	Ex	Good
COLORING BOOK	Saalfield	1965	25	14	8

A beautiful family portrait graces the cover of this coloring book.

			Mint	Ex	Good
COLORING BOOK	Artcraft		70	60	50

Number 4331.

			Mint	Ex	Good
COLORFORMS	Colorforms	1965	65	35	20

This set had a sketch of the living room on the inside along with the traditional vinyl body parts for creating that special scene. The box lid features an unusual photo of the family gathered around Lurch's harpsichord.

			Mint	Ex	Good
DOLLS	Remco	1964	1,000	550	300

These figures are a very rare find. Three dolls were made—Lurch, Morticia and Fester. They came in windowed boxes with a green frame. The dolls were less than five inches tall with oversized rubbery heads and rooted hair (where applicable).

			Mint	Ex	Good
FESTER'S MYSTERY LIGHT BULB	**Unknown**	**64/66**	**75**	**40**	**22**

Another magic store novelty, this light bulb was supposed to light by magic when you put it in your mouth. Unfortunately, my silly mother always told me not to put battery operated toys in my mouth, so I never was allowed to try it. Look for a close-up of Fester's head on the box.

GAME, BOARD	**Ideal**	**1964**	**50**	**27**	**15**

The game board featured seven squares, each dedicated to a family member with their own path to the center square. Board art is on the cutesy side, but the lid shows a nice long shot of the family house with a group photo on the right and a mischievous long-legged skeleton under the logo.

GAME, CARD	**Milton Bradley**	**1965**	**75**	**45**	**30**

Another oversized card game by MB. It's kind of a spooky "Go Fish." This dealer included a card autographed by Wednesday herself.

			Mint	Ex	Good
MODEL, HOUSE	**Aurora**	**1964**	**850**	**470**	**255**

This model began as another famous James Bama painting from Aurora. Reproductions of his art can be found at toy shows today. This is a particularly clever model that came, to quote the box, "complete with ghosts." The ghosts were set up on a contraption that looks like a mug tree with a handle. By building the house over the top, only the handle protruded from the front. By manipulating this lever you could make the ghosts bob around in the windows. Another ghost opens the front door and comes out on the porch. This working mechanism was very unusual for Aurora. This time the model is as cool as the box.

PUPPETS	**Ideal**	**1964**	**100**	**55**	**30**

Ideal made a set of puppets with hand-shaped fabric bodies and plastic heads. The fabric is printed with a sketch of the character's body and is labeled with the character's name. (Watch the Dick Van Dyke episode about the government spy and you'll see two of the puppets hanging on Ritchie's bedroom closet door.)

THING BANK	**Unknown**	**64/66**	**60**	**33**	**18**

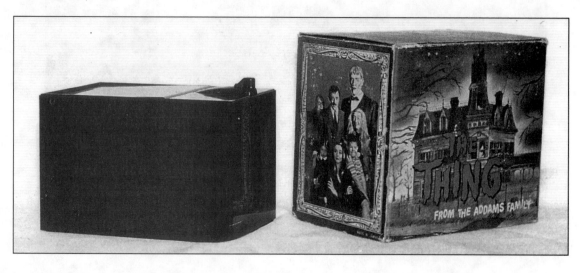

THING BANK (cont.)

This generic hand in a box bank was sold at many a trick store and boardwalk arcade. It was basically a black cube with a slot for a coin. Inserting a coin would activate the bank, and a pale hand would shoot out and steal your money. The cardboard display box had a very eerie shot of the Addams house with the words "The Thing" covering most of it.

	Mint	Ex	Good
VIEW-MASTER (#B486)	125	106	—

It's the basic three wheel bit, but this one is pretty rare. Great cover shot adds to the value.

**In the early seventies, *The Addams Family* was released as a Saturday morning cartoon. Several toys were generated to commemorate this series and should not be confused with collectibles from the original series.

THE MUNSTERS

September 1964 - September 1966

When Boris Karloff created his version of the Frankenstein monster, audiences were terrified. Women screamed and some even fainted. When Fred Gwynne created his version of the man-made monster, the only screams were in fits of laughter. Herman Munster may have looked like his movie counterpart, but inside he was all heart. (Of course, whose heart we'll never know.) Herman was a hard worker earning a living at the funeral home of Gateman, Goodbury and Graves, and more than anything he was a devoted family man. His charming wife Lily, played by the lovely Yvonne DeCarlo, always tried to put on her best, albeit pale, face when entertaining company. Son Eddie (Butch Patrick) was an exemplary student excelling in the sciences, particularly when it came to lab work and dissections. Living with the family was the poor unfortunate niece Marilyn (played by both Beverly Owen and Pat Priest), who spent her life bemoaning the curse of being born blond and built. Finishing off the family was dear Grandpa, Lily's father and resident vampire, mad scientist, and all-around prankster, played by Al Lewis. The family resided at 1313 Mockingbird Lane in Mockingbird Heights with their beloved pets, Spot, a dragon-like creature that lived under the stairs, Igor, the family bat, and that ever-annoying cuckoo clock Raven, whose voice was supplied by the famous Mel Blanc. The house can still be seen on the tour at Universal Studios.

Though it is often compared to its spooky ooky neighbor *The Addams Family*, *The Munsters* actually had more in common with its cartoon cousin *The Flintstones*. The comedy in *The Munsters* came from one reoccurring thread: Herman tries to do something great, Grandpa tries to help him out, and everything goes haywire. Episodes played hard on slapstick humor with plenty of pratfalls and funny fights. Remember Herman moonlighting as a wrestler to get money for Eddie's college education? Or Herman studying to be a private detective while Lily thinks he's seeing another woman? Or Herman becoming a baseball player, a race car driver, a basketball star ... the list goes on and on. Unlike *The Addams Family*, with its portrayal of a family that works together in a pinch, the Munsters were constantly at odds with each other. With Herman's childish tantrums, Grandpa's scheming, and Lily's constant scolding, it often seemed that little Eddie was the most grown up figure in the bunch. Given all that, the Munsters do share something with the Addamses: both shows debuted a week apart in the same year, and both were canceled in the same week two years later.

These days the Munsters are still turning up on TV and on the toy shelf. The show spawned two movies and a remake TV series, *The Munsters Today*, with an all new cast. Al Lewis and Butch Patrick can be seen donning costume and make-up every Halloween to host Munster Marathons. While you're at the mall, check out Fred Gwynne's series of children's books which he wrote and illustrated. Stop at the used record store to search for a copy of Butch Patrick's record called "What Ever Happened to Eddie," and if you're in New York, you have to stop and eat at Grandpa's Italian restaurant in Greenwich Village. Only then will you be a true *Munsters* fan.

Munsters Collectibles

			Mint	Ex	Good
CAR	**AMT**	**1964**	**250**	**140**	**75**

This is a pretty rare toy car that was produced by model company AMT. The car is a nicely detailed version of Barris's famous Munster Koach and does not require assembly.

COLORFORMS	**Colorforms**	**1965**	**150**	**82**	**45**

The usual Colorforms set with a living room scene on which to stick your vinyl body parts. Nice photo cover on the box.

COLORING BOOKS	**Whitman**		**75**	**65**	**50**

Numbers 1149 and 1648. Price is for each.

			Mint	Ex	Good
COMICS	**Gold Key**	**1965-68**	50	22	7

Sixteen issues were released over a three-year period. The back covers could be used as pin-ups for teens' bedroom walls.

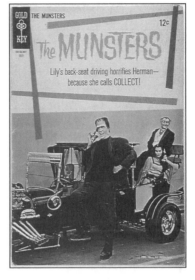

DOLL, HERMAN	**Mattel**	**1964**	175	100	55

This Herman came with a soft cloth body and a plastic head. It had a pull string and a voice box so it could talk. Except for the body, this doll is identical to the Mattel puppet.

DOLLS	**Remco**	**1964**	100	40	22

This set of Munsters dolls included Grandpa, Lily and Herman. The dolls were about five to six inches tall with rubbery bodies and oversized heads. The dolls came in a red tinted box with a clear plastic window in the front. Remco also made an identical set of Addams Family dolls. Nothing like covering all your bases.

DOLLS	**Ideal**	**1965**	75	40	22

This series of dolls was called Mini-Monsters. They were childlike versions of Herman, Lily and Eddie, and while they were not actually sold as Munsters dolls, the likeness is unmistakable.

			Mint	Ex	Good
GAME, BOARD	**Hasbro**	**1965**	**125**	**70**	**40**

The Munster's Picnic game has large color graphics on the board showing Herman and his bunch in the park. The board is very unusual and is identical in style to the other two games from Hasbro.

GAME, BOARD	**Hasbro**	**1965**	**125**	**70**	**40**

The Munsters Drag Race Game was just like above except the graphics show Herman drag racing in the famous Munster Koach.

GAME, BOARD	**Hasbro**	**1965**	**125**	**70**	**40**

Munsters Masquerade Party Game is the third from Hasbro. Again, large color graphics show the family at play in Grandpa's lab.

GAME, BOARD	**Milton Bradley**	**1966**	**150**	**95**	**65**
GAME, CARD	**Milton Bradley**	**1964**	**30**	**17**	**9**

Another example of the popularity of card games in the sixties. The box features a very playful graphic of the family playing the game.

GUM CARDS	**Leaf**	**1966**	**125**	**70**	**40**

Seventy-two gum cards comprise this black and white set of Munsters Gum Cards. Each card features a photo from the show with a funny caption. The backs have Munsters Mumbles, which were joke-style lines from the series. The set also came with sixteen colorful cartoon stickers.

LUNCH BOX	**King Seeley**	**1965**	**125**	**70**	**40**

LUNCH BOX (cont.)

Colorful box art drawn by Nick Lo Bianco shows Herman in the electric chair about to be "turned on" by his wife Lily on one side, and the family heading out on a car trip on the other. This square metal box is done with lots of pink and orange, giving it a real comic book look. The thermos is green with portraits of the family all around.

		Mint	Ex	Good
MODEL, DIORAMA Aurora	1964	850	470	255

The Munsters Family at Home kit is one of the most sought after kits by Aurora collectors. It is an extremely detailed diorama in 1:16 scale that finds Lily knitting in her coffin seat with Herman relaxing in his electric lazy boy. Little Eddie is seated in front of a roaring fire with his precious wolf wolf doll in hand. Best part? Check out the pet rabbit on top of the TV set. Talk about a great pair of rabbit ears. This model has been known to sell at auction for upwards of $2,000.

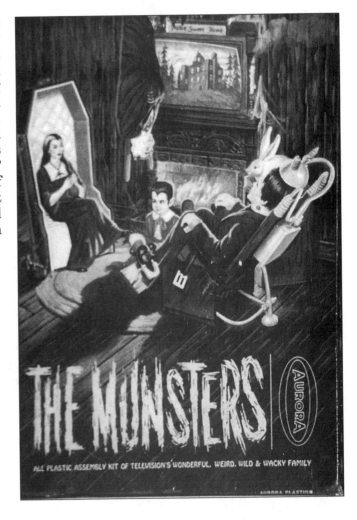

		Mint	Ex	Good
MODEL, KOACH AMT	1964	150	82	45

This replica of the family car is a poor stepchild to the great Aurora models. No fancy artwork, but the model is a good find nonetheless.

		Mint	Ex	Good
MODEL, DRAGULA AMT	1964	150	82	45

The same as above with this version of a drag race vehicle.

			Mint	Ex	Good
PAPER DOLLS	**Whitman**	**1966**	**60**	**33**	**18**

Every little girl's favorite toy, a set of cut-out figures with various costumes. Paper dolls should be uncut to demand full price.

			Mint	Ex	Good
PUPPET, HERMAN	**Mattel**	**1964**	**150**	**82**	**45**

Mattel, the inventors of the talking doll, put their genius to work on two versions of talking Hermans. This one is a hand puppet with a cloth body, and hard rubber head and hands. The voice mechanism inside is quite heavy, making the puppet difficult to hold, but if you find one that still works, buy it.

			Mint	Ex	Good
PUPPETS, HAND	**Unknown**	**1964**	**100**	**55**	**30**

These odd little puppets were made of cloth with a plastic head. Their costumes are painted on the front of the glove with the character names underneath.

PUZZLE	**Whitman**	**1965**	**40**	**22**	**12**

The ever popular jigsaw puzzle was designed for the Munster family. The one hundred-piece puzzle formed a cartoonish picture of the Munsters having a family sing-along.

VIEW-MASTER (#B481)			**125**	**106**	**—**

Three round discs with a little paper book. Fairly rare and really fun.

FAMILY AFFAIR

September 1966 - September 1971

It doesn't sound much like a plot for a comedy. Three children, orphaned when their parents are killed in a car accident, are sent to live with an uncle they hardly know. A bachelor, nonetheless, who spends his days either flying all over the world as a consulting engineer, or wining and dining the ladies. Oh, yeah, lots of laughs. Well, it's true. *Family Affair* brought that odd little group together in a wholesome, heartwarming family comedy, something that had almost gone out of style in the sixties. Bill Davis (Brian Keith) was the unlucky uncle who inherited custody of his brother's children. He lived in a stylish Manhattan high-rise apartment with his Gentleman's Gentleman Mr. French, played by the impeccable Sebastian Cabot. Arriving on the scene one night was fifteen-year-old Cissy, played by Kathy Garver, and those nauseatingly cute twins Buffy and Jody, played by Anissa Jones and Johnnie Whitaker. Bill expected to keep them for a week. He got them for life. And so it began, two men learning to care for three children. Pâté de foie gras was replaced with hot dogs and beans. Saturdays on the terrace became mornings at the zoo and the word "quiet" was banished from their vocabulary. The first episode is actually a bit of a tearjerker. Brian Keith does an excellent job as the lost but willing substitute parent, and French, with his overbearing English attitude, softens to an overstuffed teddy bear after a bit.

Family Affair looked at life in a way that was very different from the family sitcoms of the fifties. No suburban ranch house with a pool and a yard. Buffy and Jody had only the park to play in. Coming home from school meant saying hello to the doorman and a ride to the upper floors. City living, especially rich city living, was not something Americans were used to watching. The children were soon laden with the best clothes, a mountain of new toys and a servant, but were they happy? NO! Buffy wanted Mrs. Beasley, an old yarn-haired rag doll with granny spectacles on her nose, Jody wanted Bill, and Cissy only wanted to be treated like an adult. Episode by episode they grew together, facing the everyday challenges of lost homework, first dates, and the always horrible "I want a pet" phase of life. It was a simple show, no great acting, no dramatic plots, never out on a limb, just life in the big city. I guarantee, the moment you see that kaleidoscope start to turn during the beginning credits, you'll feel warm all over again. Give it a try next chance you get.

The collectibles for the series are all based on Buffy and Jody, who were six years old at the start of the series. Mrs. Beasley, Buffy's doll, actually gets more press than any of the characters.

Family Affair Collectibles

			Mint	Ex	Good
COLORING BOOK	**Whitman**	**1968**	**15**	**8**	**5**

A sketch of Buffy and Mrs. Beasley dominates the cover of this Family Affair coloring book. Insets of the whole cast form a circle around them.

COLORING BOOK	**Western/Whitman**	**1969**	**15**	**8**	**5**

The Buffy and Jody coloring book has a cute cover of the children flying a kite in the park while Mr. French walks behind carrying Mrs. Beasley.

DOLL	**Mattel**	**1967**	**100**	**55**	**30**

Buffy and Mrs. Beasley came together in a window box. Buffy was a six-inch-tall vinyl doll with wires to make her poseable. She carried a three-inch version of her famous Mrs. Beasley (making it a doll of a doll, I guess). Buffy looks very much like the Tutti doll Mattel was making for their Barbie line around the same time. Intentional or coincidental? You decide.

			Mint	Ex	Good
DOLL	**Mattel**	**1967**	**75**	**40**	**22**

This Buffy doll was part of Mattel's talking doll line. She is about a foot tall, with blonde hair in those corkscrew curls and a red and white dress. Even though she does resemble Anissa Jones, she has that unmistakable facial expression of a Mattel doll from the sixties.

			Mint	Ex	Good
DOLL, MRS. BEASLEY	**Mattel**	**1968**	**200**	**110**	**60**

This "life-size" replica of Mrs. Beasley had Mattel's patented talk box inside her soft blue polka dot body. Owning her makes you feel like a real TV star.

GAME, BOARD	**Whitman**	**1971**	**30**	**17**	**9**

This game is unusual since it is made by Whitman, a company that normally sticks to puzzles and coloring books. The lid shows a nice light sketch of Buffy and Jody running in the park. One can imagine that the game itself was designed for young children. It isn't Stratego, I'll tell you that.

LUNCH BOX	**King Seeley**	**1969**	**50**	**27**	**15**

Square metal lunch box shows a sketch of Buffy and Cissy having a birthday party for … you guessed it, Mrs. Beasley. Odd that there are only two candles on the cake, since she doesn't look a day under sixty-three.

PAPER DOLLS	**Whitman**	**1968**	**30**	**17**	**9**

Buffy paper dolls featured Anissa Jones and that darn Mrs. Beasley on the cover of the booklet. These are collectible by fans of the show as well as paper doll collectors, so they're a double whammy.

			Mint	Ex	Good
PAPER DOLLS	**Whitman**	**1970**	**30**	**17**	**9**

Whitman also released paper dolls in boxes, including a "Buffy & Jody" set with a sketch of the freckle-faced twins on the box, and a "Family Affair" set with a tallest-to-shortest sketch of the entire family on the box.

VIEW-MASTER (#B571)	**GAF**	**1966**	**25**	**21**	**8**

You know the drill by now. Three reels, little book, it's a View-Master, right.

THE MONKEES

September 1966 - August 1968

Do you know what you get if you nail little metal bottle tops all over your living room floor? Easy, you get the sensation of walking on 'ittle, met'l, bot'l tops. Said with the appropriate Cockney accent, of course! Hey, Hey, they were the Monkees and the music business would never be the same again. The whole insane idea came from the heads of Bob Rafelson and Bert Schneider. The two Hollywood freelancers were hoping to make some fast cash in TV and maybe create a small phenomenon along the way. They came up with a show about four boys in a rock band. It would be cool, hip, psychedelic, and as an added bonus, the weekly tunes would reach thousands before ever hitting vinyl. So they placed a now infamous ad in the Hollywood trades asking for actors to audition. They received 437 responses, including some from such musical stars as Paul Williams, Harry Nilsson and Stephen Stills. It is rumored that even Charles Manson tried his hand at becoming a Monkee. In the end, it was only Mike Nesmith who came via the ad. Davy Jones and Mickey Dolenz were already veteran actors at the ages of nineteen and twenty respectively. Mickey had starred in TV's *Circus Boy* at the age of ten. Peter Tork came "word of mouth" from his friend and co-Monkee hopeful Stills. The Raybert production team hired the musical duo of Boyce and Hart, known as two of the fastest songwriters in town. They were also frequent guests on sitcoms like *Bewitched* and *I Dream of Jeannie*. The team penned the show's first big hit, "The Last Train to Clarksville." Rock and roll guru Don Kirshner was also cut in for a piece of the pie. Actually, when it came to the Monkees' sound, Kirshner had more to do with it than any of the four actors. He wrote more than twenty songs, had the music recorded, and supervised the boys' voice-overs in the studio. Then, unhappy with the unpolished sound of the four, he used high-tech recording equipment to make the vocals sound the way he wanted. The Monkees were truly nothing but tape and electronics, but the computer-generated sound was selling millions and it might have gone on that way until someone let the secret loose.

When word got out that the Monkees didn't do their own performing, the group had to put out or get out. So began marathon sessions with the musical producers, learning how to play and sing, and how to mimic the sound that had been created in the studio. They hit Hawaii with their very first concert and when they stepped on the stage, all the work didn't matter. The crowd screamed from beginning to end, covering any sounds made by the four tired actors. Monkeemania had begun. Early episodes of the series were full of good-natured clowning. The show had a directing style all its own, using fast cutaways, slow motion effects, sudden zooms—anything for a laugh. The boys were free and wild and comfortable to watch. They were innocent in an era of drugs and war. As the series progressed, so did The Monkees as a group. They matured and changed. Their music went from bubble gum ditties like "I'm a Believer" to hippie-style protest tunes. "Daily Nightly" can't be anything but a drug induced trip, and "She Hangs Out" smacks of the sexual revolution. Their costumes went from Carnaby Street Mod to flower power ponchos and Nehru jackets. The humor took a turn toward biting and bizarre, leaving audiences yearning for those four fresh-faced boys who were determined to take the music world by storm. It would seem that Dolenz, Tork, Nesmith and Jones were hired as actors, but they soon fell victim to their own publicity, believing they were the hit rock group The Monkees. The group set out to prove they had talent beyond the creative production team that put the show on the air every week. Their hope of becoming the next Beatles soon died. After the release of their none-too-successful movie *HEAD*, the group began to fall apart one by one until only Davy and Mickey were singing together. Here's one last equation: What's four Monkees minus two Monkees? No Monkees.

Monkees Collectibles

			Mint	Ex	Good
BADGES	Donruss	1967	100	55	30

These award-shaped photo stickers came packaged like their big brother the bubble gum card. There were forty-four different stickers. They are particularly rare since most girls peeled and stuck them long ago.

BOOKS	Popular Library	1967	—	5	—

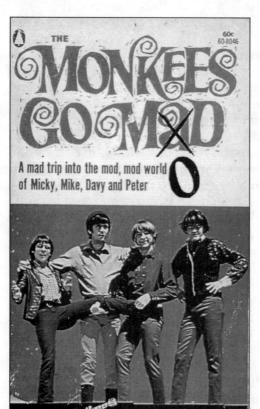

The Monkees Go Mod was a mad trip into the mod, mod world of Mickey, Mike, Davy, and Peter.

			Mint	Ex	Good
CAR	**Corgi**	**1967**	**400**	**220**	**120**

This die cast metal replica of The Monkeemobile is a high ticket item mainly because of the value of Corgi cars alone. As with everything the company makes, this car is highly detailed right down to the tiny Monkees logo on the door.

Here's a comic book's ad for the Mighty Miniatures series by Corgi. Notice the Monkeemobile's kooky design.

FLIP BOOKS	**Topps**	**1967**	**80**	**45**	**25**

Another five-cent item from the Woolworth's counter. These tiny flip books came in sixteen different styles. Each consisted of several photos that created a story when flipped quickly. (Not exactly George Lucas's Industrial Light and Magic, but cool for the sixties.)

GAME, BOARD	**Transogram**	**1967**	**75**	**40**	**22**

Even though this game is very unusual and fairly rare, the price reflects the general lack of interest in board game buying. The board itself was cleverly designed as a piece of music, challenging the players into gathering all of the notes they needed to complete the theme song. Quite cute. It really should sell for more than it does.

			Mint	Ex	Good
GUITAR	**Mattel**	**1966**	**100**	**55**	**30**

Here was an easy deal for Mattel. They took an old plastic guitar, probably a Mickey Mouse Club leftover, and stuck a sticker with a cartoon picture of the boys on it. I bet it sold millions.

GUM CARDS	**Donruss**	**66/67**	**60**	**33**	**18**

Incredible as it may seem, Donruss released four different sets of Monkees cards, each featuring forty-four photo cards. The first series was done in a sepia tone with white borders around the cards. The other three sets were done in color with white, yellow and pink frames used respectively. The fourth set is labeled "More of the Monkees" and its box is the only one done with a photo rather than a sketch.

LUNCH BOX	**King Seeley**	**1967**	**200**	**110**	**60**

This vinyl lunch box came with a photo of the four Monkees (just their heads actually), but their bodies are pictured on the thermos. Don't confuse the soft vinyl style with the hard plastic that is used today. The vinyl ones from this era were easily cut or torn, making them just as valuable as their metal friends from the sixties. One would tend to think that vinyl was used for the Monkees box so it would resemble the vinyl 45 record boxes that were all the rage at the time.

			Mint	Ex	Good
MODEL, MONKEEMOBILE	**MPC**	**1967**	**100**	**55**	**30**

This plastic model was a fairly well detailed replica of Barris's famous funny car. The box shows a picture of the finished car over a shot of the Monkees. Although the box art can't compete with the Aurora paintings of the era, it is still a very nice piece for model collectors as well as Monkee collectors.

PUPPET	**Mattel**	**1966**	**140**	**77**	**42**

This innovative puppet was part of Mattel's stable of talking toys. The cloth puppet came with four plastic heads (one for each finger, almost) and a pull string in the bottom corner. The voice box in this thing was so heavy no kid under fifteen would have a chance in the world of making it work. Still, it is one of the best finds, especially if you find one with the voice box still working, but even a non-working model sells for $50 and up.

PUZZLE, JIGSAW	**Unknown**	**1967**	**50**	**27**	**15**

This jigsaw puzzle contained 340 pieces with a finished size of 17" x 11". It featured the guys playing a gig with a young girl sporting a perfect flip hairdo in the right foreground. Probably a British import.

VIEW-MASTER (#B493)			**30**	**26**	**—**

The only thing missing is the music. Maybe if you listen to a record while you watch.

GET SMART

September 1965 - September 1970

It was the old copy-a-spy-show-but-make-it-into-a-comedy-show trick and boy did it have us fooled. In its first year, *Get Smart* won more rating points than the *Ed Sullivan Show*. By the end of its run, the series had won seven Emmys. By 1968, the set had been visited by eight presidents. Or would you believe five presidents? One president and six boy scouts? With Maxwell Smart on the job, it's hard to know what to believe!

Get Smart was the brain child of famed comedians and movie makers Buck Henry and Mel Brooks. They brought their off sense of humor and penchant for satire to the small screen in a way that had never been done before. Don Adams came to the series straight from his role on *The Bill Dana Show* and he brought with him some of his favorite quips, such as Smart's famous "Would you believe ..." line. Along for the wild ride was Barbara Feldon, whose previous fame had come from her work as a Revlon model. "99" started out as Max's partner in work and ended up as his partner for life when they married in the fourth season. (Soon to be followed by the birth of triplets.) It began each week behind all those doors and down that secret elevator in the head-quarters of CONTROL. Here our agents prepared to do battle with the likes of KAOS, the organization devoted to meanness and nastiness. (Just a bit like the U.N.C.L.E./ THRUSH setup, wouldn't you say?) CONTROL was run by The Chief, played by Edward Platt. His appearances offered Don Adams a chance to utter one of most quoted lines of all time, "Sorry about that, Chief." And did he have a lot to be sorry about. Poor Edward Platt was constantly on the receiving end of Smart's bumbling. At least once an episode viewers could count on him to be spilled on, tripped over, or smacked on the head thanks to Smart. Not that Max had a corner on clumsy. Except for 99, most of CONTROL's agents were none too swift. Remember Hymie the Robot played by Dick Gautier? He had the unfortunate habit of taking everything literally. Ask Hymie to give you a hand and you'll likely receive a set of fingers—no arm included. Larabee (Robert Karvellas) was The Chief's right-hand man and possibly the only agent more bumbling than Smart. Agent 13, played by Dave Ketchum, was a master of disguise, usually inanimate. Look for 13 inside a mailbox or in the engine of your car. Lucky for CONTROL, the agents for KAOS weren't much higher on the scholarly scale. Bernie Koppell made his mark as Siegfried the stereotypical German baddie from the limbs of The Red Baron's family tree. Then there was The Groovy Guru, played by Larry Storch, all wound up in a plan to take over the minds of America's teens. And what would a spy show be without its specialized gadgets? Long before the invention of the car phone, Max was outfitted with his famous shoe phone. It was always convenient, but could be deadly if worn on a rainy day. Secret conversations demanded The Cone of Silence, a half bubble that came down from the ceiling, encasing both parties in plastic. Once in place, no one outside could hear their conversation. Unfortunately, no one inside the cone could hear either. So much for security.

Henry and Brooks were big on parody and puns. Check out some of these titles: "The Mess of Adrian Listenger," "The Treasure of C. Errol Madre," "Spy, Spy, Birdie" and my personal favorite, "Tequilla Mockingbird," which comes off as shades of *The Maltese Falcon*. Hey, if you're gonna steal, steal from the best.

Get Smart Collectibles

				Mint	Ex	Good
BOOK		**Tempo Books**	**1965**	—	**7**	—

T-103

An original novel about NBC television's hottest, most hilarious super-spy, MAXWELL SMART, Agent 86 for CONTROL

TEMPO BOOKS 60¢

GET SMART!

By William Johnston

Tempo Books produced several Maxwell Smart books, as well as one based upon Rod Serling's *The Twilight Zone*.

COLORING BOOK	**Saalfield**	**1965**	**50**	**18**	**6**

Get Smart, Maxwell Smart that is! Or so sayeth the cover of the book. Look for a cute shot of Max all tangled up with his dog on the cover.

			Mint	Ex	Good
COMICS	**Dell**	**66-67**	**40**	**18**	**6**

Dell at it again with nice photo covers on issues 1-7.

GAME, BOARD	**Ideal**	**1965**	**50**	**27**	**15**

The Get Smart Exploding Time Bomb Game came with a spring-loaded time bomb. The object was to build a picture of a KAOS agent before you went up in smoke. Great adventure for tiny terrorists in training. Nice box graphics with Max in the middle of a mess, as usual.

GAME, CARD	**Ideal**	**1966**	**40**	**22**	**12**

Ideal also tried its hand at card games. Look for that silly old dog on the cover again.

			Mint	Ex	Good
GAME, ELECTRONIC	Lisbeth Whiting Co.	1965	75	40	22

A nice twist on the old board game, this one came with electrodes that you touched to the correct answer on a punch card. The battery operated game would light up when you answered correctly.

			Mint	Ex	Good
GUM CARDS	Topps	1966	100	55	30

This is a very odd one indeed. The bubble gum cards themselves were black and white photos from the series, but came in a sheet of two that had to be broken apart, creating cards of odd sizes. The "Secret Agent Kits" included a set of punch-out disguises that were included one in a pack. The sixty-six cards in the set had quizzes on the backs with the answers hidden in a scratch-off box. Don't be misled by the quiz. It's not trivia, simply a collection of old children's riddles such as, "When the clock strikes 13, what time is it?" (Time to get a new clock, you fool.)

			Mint	Ex	Good
LUNCH BOX	King Seeley	1966	100	55	30

This lunch box was done with cartoonish artwork on all sides of Max and 99 at work. The likenesses aren't very good.

			Mint	Ex	Good
MODEL, CAR	AMT	1967	75	40	22

Replica model of the car from *Get Smart*. Box art is rather odd, with the car pictured over radiating circles and a montage of photos on the right. The car itself is not too thrilling. Buy this one for the box.

RADIO/LIPSTICK	MPC	1966	75	40	22

What lady agent would be caught dead without her lipstick on! Well, now you can listen to the latest news and look beautiful too, with this lipstick radio combo. The set came with an earpiece to allow you to listen to your lipstick in secret.

RADIO/PEN	MPC	1966	50	27	15

This fountain pen was a real working AM radio. Boxed set came with an earpiece and clip for neighborhood spying. Strange, but the box says no batteries or electricity are needed. How the radio could run without either of these must be the secret.

THE BEVERLY HILLBILLIES

September 1962 - September 1971

So, here's this guy, right. He's dirt poor, living in a tiny cabin in the backwoods of Bugtussle. One day he's a shootin' for some food, when up through the ground comes a bubblin' crude. Oil, that is. You know—black gold, Texas Tea. So, anyway, the next thing you know, Jed, he's like a millionaire, so his kin folks say, "Jed, move away from there." They say, "Californy is the place you oughta be." Gosh darn if they didn't load up their truck and move to Beverly—Hills that is, swimmin' pools, movie stars .... That kind of says it all, don't it? Actually, *The Beverly Hillbillies* gets the prize for the best set up titles of any show. Even though you've heard it a million times, it's still easy listenin'. Part of the credit goes to that champion bluegrass team of Earl Flatt and Lester Scruggs. Along with a pickin' and a singin' the theme, Flatt and Scruggs made an annual pilgrimage to the show, appearing in at least one episode per year.

The series, which was created and produced by Paul Henning, starred Buddy Ebsen as Jed Clampett, unwilling millionaire. Ebsen, who had quite a following as a movie hoofer (that's dancer for you novices), created a character that was warm, friendly and likable to a fault. He was usually the straight man, setting up lines for his fellow actors to bounce off of. Like Irene Ryan, who played Granny. This lovely lady let her hair down each week as the crotchety old woman who longed to go back to the hills. Beside her were Max Baer, Jr. as Jed's not-too-swift son Jethro, and Donna Douglas as Jed's niece Elly May. Max Baer, whose father was a champion fighter, played his character with great enthusiasm, if not a lot of brains. Jethro, who was educated clean through the third grade, really liked the Hollywood lifestyle and always had his heart set on some new career week after week. Like the time he wanted to be a master spy, or a movie director, or best yet, a brain surgeon. Lumbering and lanky, Jethro could still find himself at the mercy of his cousin Elly May. The word "tomboy" was invented for Elly, with her rope-tied blue jeans, her yard full of animals and her penchant for climbing trees. Elly's menagerie included everything from ducks, to cats, to bears in one episode, and let's not forget the family dog, Duke, the bleary-eyed bloodhound. Backing up the family were two unforgettable characters, Milburn Drysdale, that money hungry banker played by Milburn Stone, and his faithful but overworked secretary, Miss Jane Hathaway, played by Nancy Kulp. Mr. Drysdale and Miss Jane gave balance to the show. It was their job to teach the Clampetts how to deal with their new lifestyle. For Drysdale it was a matter of keeping Jed happy so he wouldn't take his money and run. For Miss Jane, what began as a job thrust upon her, became a welcome challenge as she grew fonder of the family, with special notice to Jethro. Week after week, the scripts revolved around the Clampetts' attempts to adjust to Beverly Hills, but more often than not, the result was forcing Beverly Hills to adjust to the Clampetts.

Beverly Hillbillies Collectibles

			Mint	Ex	Good
CAR	Ideal	1963	600	330	180

This replica of the Clampetts' truck was made of plastic and had a spring-wound motor. It included figures of the family and a few accessory pieces. Pretty rare.

COLORFORMS	Colorforms	1963	100	55	30

Very nice set. The play surface was a drawing of the front hall of the mansion with the sweeping staircase. Colorform pieces were included for all members of the family.

COLORING BOOK	Watkins	1964	35	30	25
COLORING SET	Standard Toykraft	1963	50	27	15

This set came with ten numbered sketches plus crayons and paints. The front of the box is a window display that shows some cute, if not terribly correct, caricatures of the family.

GAME, BOARD	Standard Toykraft	1963	50	27	15

Cute board game has actual photos of the family superimposed over a cartoon. The left side of the box clearly displays the CBS eye, lest you forget what channel it ran on.

GAME, CARD	Milton Bradley	1963	50	27	15

Another one of MB's famous card game sets.

			Mint	Ex	Good
GUM CARDS	**Topps**	1963	100	55	30

Set of sixty-six photo cards have captions at the bottom. The backs have Hillbilly Gags, along with another reminder to watch the show every Wednesday on CBS. (Could have been expensive if they had changed the night it aired.) The wrappers have a rather poor sketch of the group, while the box has the exact same picture in photo form.

LUNCH BOX	**Aladdin**	1963	75	40	22

Another nice Elmer Lenhardt box, embossed and trimmed in red. One side shows a very clear detailed scene of the family departing the mansion in their truck. Notice the flat tire, the leaking radiator, and Duke hiding behind Jed's hat. The back side of the box shows Jed and kin back in Bugtussle just after the oil strike. (Kind of a before and after box.)

PUNCH-OUT BOOK	**Whitman**	1964	30	17	9

Cute punch-out book with figures, car and mansion. Cover has a nice sketch of the family with Jed prominent in the foreground.

PUZZLE, JIGSAW	**Jaymar**	1963	50	27	15

Boxed puzzle featured a nice photo of the family with cute graphics around the logo.

			Mint	Ex	Good
PUZZLE, TRAY	**Milton Bradley**	**1963**	**50**	**27**	**15**

Set of three tray puzzles, each with a photo from the show.

			Mint	Ex	Good
VIEW-MASTER (#B570)	**GAF**	**1963**	**35**	**30**	**—**

The usual—round wheels, pictures, little book. You get the idea.

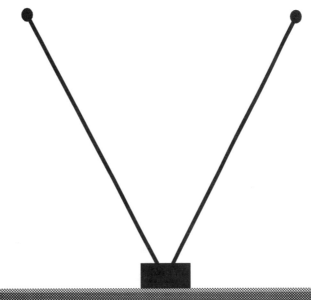

THE FINAL FRONTIER:

SCIENCE FICTION ON TELEVISION

A single wide-winged spacecraft careens past a star gone nova, straight into the jaws of a gelatinous, undulating protoplasmic energy being. We hold our breath as the pilot pivots right, firing off a burst of antimatter beams. The monster's flesh takes on a reddish glow and we know implosion is near. Our hero in the wide wing fires one last burst, leads his ship into a graceful tuck and roll, and is free. Smashing the button for overdrive, he cuts into hyperspace as the creature is sucked into itself, leaving behind nothing but a great black hole. All in a day's work—in outer space, that is.

Science fiction has been a part of our lives since Jules Verne penned his tales at the turn of the century, but sci-fi on television has gone in and out of vogue over the years. In the fifties, movie serial spin-offs like *Buck Rogers* and *Flash Gordon* captured our imagination. Cardboard ships flew on not-so-invisible wires and planetary explosions were created with the use of Fourth of July sparklers. Space was full of evil aliens trying to take over the Earth and the world was generally saved by a guy wearing tights. With advances in special effects technology and a rising level of sophistication in the TV viewing audience, we made our way to the likes of *Star Trek: The Next Generation*. Now the ships are highly detailed models photographed by a computer and the bad guys aren't always from another planet.

It wasn't until the mid-sixties that we saw sci-fi as something other than children's fare. It was in 1963 that we got our first glimpse of *The Outer Limits* and it changed the way we looked at our world, our place in the universe, and ourselves. Suddenly our vision of the future was colored by images from *Star Trek* and *Battlestar Galactica*. Aliens ran the gamut from the silly lobster man on *Voyage to the Bottom of the Sea*, to genetically advanced members of society on *Alien Nation*. As much as the American viewing public liked their sci-fi TV, toy manufacturers loved it all the more. Science fiction gave toy designers a chance to let their imaginations run wild. Fantastic creatures, grandiose spaceships, and a whole arsenal of new-age weapons were developed in plastic, metal, and cardboard, including robots that walked, ships that talked, and brain-eating monsters that oozed slime from their mouths. Remco made every kid a potential astronaut with its *Lost in Space* helmet set, while Ideal sent us into *The Twilight Zone* with its board game. And there has never been a more merchandised property than *Star Trek*. From the original series to *Voyager*, *Trek* toys have held a spot on the toy store shelves for over thirty years and have become the mainstay of small toy companies such as Galoob (with their Micro Machines) and Playmates (with their line of figures). So the next time freeway traffic gets you down, pull out your authentic first season *Star Trek* communicator and issue that famous command, "Beam me up, Scotty." After all, escapism is at the heart of science fiction.

LOST IN SPACE

September 15, 1965 - September 11, 1968

"Warning! Warning! Danger, Will Robinson." With that we are off on a journey through spectacular action, fantastic monsters, and endless fun—we are hopelessly *Lost in Space*. In 1965, the Space Family Robinson took off in the Jupiter II with hopes of becoming the first family to colonize outer space. Guy Williams was the stalwart Professor John Robinson, four-star genius and understanding dad. Guy was already known to TV fans as Disney's masked avenger, Zorro. Straight from her role as Timmy's mom on Lassie, June Lockhart was on board as Maureen Robinson, the Donna Reed of outer space. Marta Kristen, a Swedish beauty, was cast as eldest daughter Judy Robinson and veteran actress Angela Cartwright played daughter Penny, the little girl determined to keep up with the boys. Billy Mumy, also a child star, was cast as the adventurous mini-brain Will Robinson. Mumy is generally known for his work on a particularly chilling episode of *The Twilight Zone* entitled "It's a Good Life." Finishing off the original crew was Major Don West, played by handsome heartthrob of the day, Mark Goddard. West was set up to be a love interest for Judy in the early episodes, but network censors found the idea of a "child" having romantic encounters in space too much to handle.

When producer/creator Irwin Allen pitched the series, it was minus the two characters that are most recognizable from the show: the robot and Dr. Smith. At the insistence of the network, both characters were added after the pilot was shot. Smith, marvelously acted by the unparalleled Jonathan Harris, was written in as the bad guy, and I do mean bad. In the second version of the pilot, Smith sabotages the Jupiter, but is trapped inside just before liftoff. Backing up Smith's plot was the beloved mechanical man simply known as Robot. Irwin Allen wanted to create the illusion of the robot being real, so no one was ever credited for the part. The unsung heroes were actor Bob May, who actually climbed inside the costume week after week, and voice-over veteran Dick Tuefeld, who provided the voice.

From their first take-off to their final landing, the Robinsons and company were constantly stumbling upon new alien life-forms and a few other lost humanoids. In the first season, which was filmed in black and white, Penny picks up a pet in the form of Debbie the Bloop, a monkey made to look alien with the use of chenille bump ears. The first season is also the era of the most well-rounded episodes, such as the two-parter entitled "The Keeper" starring Michael Rennie. By the second season, Irwin's usual passion for color and humor began to take over as costumes and sets were splashed in orange and pink. Stars Williams and Lockhart soon found themselves pushed aside in favor of the triangle of Will, Smith, and The Robot. An increasing number of plots surrounded Smith's scheming his way to riches, taking Will along for the ride. By the third season, *Lost in Space* had spiraled down into the depths of silliness with visits to a hippie planet, an intergalactic Miss Universe pageant, and the infamous Great Vegetable Rebellion. But don't switch off the set just yet. Smack in the middle of the season is a fantastically dark and evil episode entitled "The Antimatter Man." This episode, which features only the regular cast, reminds us of how good *Lost in Space* can be.

Even after thirty years, *Lost in Space* is held in high regard by a large and devoted fan following. As children, it was everything we dreamed of—gallivanting through the heavens, firing ray guns, hanging out with robots, and escaping from monsters—and more often than not, the kids saved the day with their inventive thinking. It is no wonder then that *Lost in Space* toys are some of the most sought after items in the TV collectibles arena today. Items such as a complete Switch and Go, mint in box, can bring several thousand dollars at auction. A set of rare Japanese Robinson dolls complete with freezing tubes can be bought for the same price as a good used car. *Lost in Space* has become synonymous with sci-fi in the sixties. *LIS* fans, warm up your charge cards.

Lost in Space Collectibles

			Mint	Ex	Good
COMIC BOOK	**Gold Key Comics**	1960s	40	25	15

Gold Key turned out a line of Space Family Robinson comic books that were based loosely on the series. And I do mean loosely.

COSTUME	**Ben Cooper**	1965	150	82	45

Your basic polyester jumpsuit done in silver with artwork of a ray gun stuck in a painted-on belt and *LIS* logo on the chest. Bet this was a hot one.

DOLLS	**Marusan**		7000	3800	2100

These awful-looking Japanese dolls came dressed in spacesuits, each in their own freezing tube with a colorful paper insert (written in Japanese). As ugly as they are, they are highly collectible since they were never released here in America. The group of seven sells for $7000.

GAME, BOARD	**Milton Bradley**	1965	75	40	22

This typical board game of the era has nice graphics on the board and a cartoon sketch of John and Maureen on the box lid.

			Mint	Ex	Good
GUM CARDS	**Topps**	**1966**	**700**	**385**	**210**

Fifty-five cards came in this black and white set. The pictures are nothing special, but single cards still sell for several dollars each. A single wrapper or the original display box go for more than $100 a piece. And buyer beware, if someone is selling a pack for under $30, they're laser reprints, not originals. With the advent of high-tech copying, it's getting hard to tell the real thing from the copy. (Is it live, or is it Memorex?)

HELMET AND GUN SET	**Remco**	**1967**	**1000**	**550**	**300**

This child-sized helmet came with a blue flashing light and logo decals that were probably added to a generic space helmet. A blue and red molded gun also came with the set. Pretty cool—and that big chunky box sure looks good under the Christmas tree.

LUNCH BOX	**King Seeley**	**1966**	**1000**	**550**	**300**

This box was one of the last dome-shaped lunch boxes made in metal. The artwork is fantastic. Deep rich colors make it a real standout. The thermos that was sold with the kit was a generic space thermos and did not bear the LIS logo at all.

		Mint	Ex	Good
MODEL, DIORAMA Aurora	1966	1200	660	360

This set is particularly rare. The first issue came with a Cyclops, figures of the Robinsons, and a mountain setting. The box art is excellent and even empty boxes sell for over $100. The kit was reissued in 1967 with a larger base and the Chariot added. With this kit, even the model instructions are being sold for $25 to $30. (Remember the pages you always threw away when you were done?)

Here's a full-page ad from a 1967 comic book describing the Lost in Space Aurora TV Hobby Kit. Cool, or what?

		Mint	Ex	Good
MODEL, JUPITER Marusan	1966	1000	650	425

This is the large version of the Japanese model kit.

		Mint	Ex	Good
MODEL, JUPITER-2 Marusan	1966	1000	650	425

Six-inch model molded in green plastic with wheels and wind-up motor.

		Mint	Ex	Good
MODEL, ROBOT Aurora	1966	800	440	240

Six-inch model of Robot with a base, originally sold for $1.00. Box alone sells for $100 and up. Beware of recastings. Many small model shops are re-creating this one and the copies are tough to tell from the originals. Buyer beware.

	Mint	Ex	Good
PUZZLES, TRAY **Milton Bradley** **1966**	**60**	**33**	**18**

Three different frame-style puzzles were released with artwork of the Robinsons and the Cyclops.

	Mint	Ex	Good
ROBOT **Remco** **1966**	**900**	**500**	**270**

This twelve-inch motorized robot is one of the most common collectibles of the series, but it is also one of the most sought after. The toy is quite stout, completely out of proportion compared to the robot on the show, and it was molded in red plastic. Still, it was used in mass quantities, painted purple in an episode of the series to represent a population of mechanical men. The box is one thing that makes the price high. Without the box, expect to pay half.

			Mint	Ex	Good
ROTO-JET GUN	**Mattel**	**1966**	**2500**	**1375**	**750**

Mattel gets the prize for this one, cutting into Remco's market just a bit. The large 24" x 14" box is covered with colorful artwork. The gun could be turned into different types of weapons by adding or detaching accessories. It also came with small round discs to shoot. This one recently sold at a Toy Scouts auction for $14,888.

SAUCER GUN	**Ahi**	**1977**	**75**	**50**	**30**

This disc shooting gun was produced by the Japanese novelty company, Ahi, years after the show went off the air.

SWITCH AND GO	**Remco**	**1966**	**2500**	**1375**	**750**

This Sears Christmas exclusive came with a very detailed chariot that ran around a track with figures and a Styrofoam Jupiter II. It was part of a line of Switch and Go toys that included Batman as well as a few generic themes. Due to the size of the toy when packaged, Sears repackaged many in plain brown boxes for mailing. Only store-bought versions came with the full color box. Boxed sets have been known to sell for over $10,000 at auction.

			Mint	Ex	Good
VIEW-MASTER AND TRU-VUE SET	**GAF**	**1967**	**75**	**64**	**—**

Both 3-D viewer sets depict the "Condemned of Space" episode from the series. The Tru-Vue set cards are rectangular but otherwise identical to the more common View-Master reels.

3-D FUN SET	**Remco**	**1966**	**1500**	**825**	**450**

This unusual board game came with three levels of cardboard supported by plastic pillars for a futuristic 3-D look. Sort of like the 3-D chess made popular on *Star Trek*. This one is tough to find since it had lots of cardboard pieces that were easily destroyed.

STAR TREK

September 1966 - June 1969

His words have become part of our vocabulary. Tribbles, Klingons, warp factor 6. Gene Roddenberry created more than a TV show; he created a page in history. *Star Trek* was not a very popular show when it premiered. It was technical. It was moralistic. It was multicultural. Three things that were rare on television at the time. Imagine a black woman on a space mission, an Oriental man as a bridge officer, and what's with the guy with the pointy ears? It was all part of Roddenberry's vision of the future. A world where everyone on the Earth has learned to get along so we have to go out into space to find trouble. And did we ever. From vicious hordes of Klingons ("Day of the Dove") to Romulans with their fancy cloaked ships ("The Enterprise Incident"), the crew of the Enterprise never lacked an enemy to fight. Remember "The Devil in the Dark," the lava rock creature that was momma to a whole nest of eggs? Or the flying pierogies that would slap themselves onto your back and drive you crazy in "Operation Annihilate?" Among my personal favorites were those hostile hippies that were looking for the "Way to Eden." Many of *Star Trek*'s best episodes revolved around the enemy within: humanity's need to avenge ("Space Seed"), our quest for eternal youth ("The Omega Glory"), our inability to deal with the issues of command ("The Doomsday Machine"). These episodes are what have given *Star Trek* life after death with its many spin-offs, movies, and novelizations.

Sitting in the command chair the first time around was Captain James T. Kirk, played by William Shatner (ever hear of him?). Actually, Shatner was no stranger to television. By the time he was hired to play Kirk he had done dozens of guest star roles on shows like *The Twilight Zone*. Right beside the captain was First Officer/Science Officer Spock from the planet Vulcan. Leonard Nimoy took on this challenging role, creating a character that will live in infamy. With his deadpan reactions and quotable quotes like, "It is not logical," it's no wonder that fans in the sixties wore buttons stating "I GROK SPOCK." DeForest Kelly, a popular Western actor, was Doctor "Bones" McCoy. (He's dead, Jim.) (Sorry, I had to.) Filling up the background were James Doohan as the ship's engineer, Scotty, George Takei as Lt. Sulu, Walter Koenig as Ensign Pavel Chekov, and the lovely Nichelle Nichols as Lt. Uhura, the communications officer.

Star Trek is arguably the most merchandised license in the world. Companies like McDonald's, Konica, and Jack-in-the-Box have all jumped on the bandwagon by using *Trek*'s universal appeal to help push their products. From a collectible standpoint, it's almost too much. Early *Trek* toys were simply that, toys made to play with. That's what makes them valuable. It is interesting to note that most of the toys were made after the series went off the air. The mid-seventies was a peak time for *Star Trek*, as Mego released its set of action figures that sell for over $100 at toy shows. Today's *Star Trek* toys are marketed with collectors in mind, with numbered, "limited" signed editions of everything from action figures to model kits. When a new item hits the shelves of Toys R Us, collectors run out and buy them by the dozen. With so many people collecting from the start, it is hard to imagine the item will have any real value in the coming years. Besides, what is the fun of collecting without the thrill of the hunt? With that said, here are just a FEW of the original *Star Trek* toys that are worth hunting for. Mr. Chekov, set a course for the outer rings of Remco, warp factor 5.

Star Trek Collectibles

			Mint	Ex	Good
BOOK	**Bantam Books**	**1967**	—	**10**	—

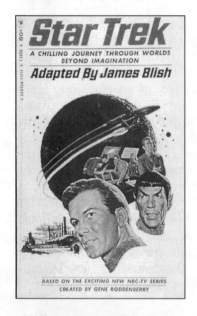

This paperback was based on the "exciting new NBC-TV series" and contained seven short stories adapted by James Blish.

COLORFORMS	**Colorforms**	**1968**	**50**	**27**	**15**

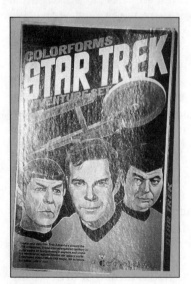

The usual bit. You know, plastic coated board with stick-on figures! Your chance to kill off the unknown crewman in the red shirt.

			Mint	Ex	Good
COLORING BOOK	**Saalfield**	**1968**	**30**	**17**	**9**

This is probably the most boring cover ever made for a coloring book. It simply uses the logo over the Enterprise and that's it.

COMMUNICATOR	**Lone Star**	**1974**	**50**	**30**	**20**

On the Inter-Space Communicator, you could either talk or listen, but not both at the same time.

COSTUME, SPOCK	**Collegeville**	**1967**	**150**	**82**	**45**

Plastic mask includes Spock ears. Synthetic jumpsuit has a picture of the Enterprise on it along with a logo and the words "Mr. Spock" written around the neckline. (Perhaps this was an old design for Starfleet uniforms.)

COSTUMES, KIRK/SPOCK	**Ben Cooper**	**1967**	**25**	**16**	**11**

Comprised merely of a tie-on jumpsuit and a mask.

			Mint	Ex	Good
FLYING SAUCER	**Remco**	**1968**	**100**	**55**	**30**

Here's your basic Frisbee with the *Star Trek* logo on it and instructions to "throw it ... it flies like a real spaceship." It's so dumb it's worth a lot!

GAME	**Ideal**	**1967**	**100**	**55**	**30**

The sophisticated artwork makes this game stand out on a shelf. Nice depiction of Kirk and Spock on the bridge watching an explosion on the view screen. (Oddly though, it looks like a World War II dogfight. Maybe it's a time warp.) Game included spaceships and various cards to help you complete your mission.

			Mint	Ex	Good
GAME	**Mego**	**1976**	**70**	**50**	**30**

The Super Phaser II Target Game may have been released in the seventies, but the artwork makes it look like it's from the sixties.

GUM CARDS   Leaf

This set of gum cards contained photographs of cast characters with poignant dialog running along the bottom. (For example, Kirk demanding that aliens return his ship, and Dr. McCoy donning an upset expression because of a "poison attack!")

			Mint	Ex	Good
LUNCH BOX	**Aladdin**	**1968**	**500**	**275**	**150**

One of the last domed lunch boxes made in metal. Art was done by Bob Burton and Elmer Lenhardt. On the back side of the box are Kirk and Spock on their knees, poised for trouble, while the Enterprise climbs high into the sky on the front. The bottom panel shows the whole crew on the bridge. The box is colorful and nicely drawn. The depiction of Spock is particularly accurate and Shatner should be happy since he looks about ten years younger on the box than in real life. Notice on the thermos that Spock is wearing the green tunic top he wears in the pilot as opposed to the blue tunic that he is wearing on the box itself.

MODEL, ENTERPRISE	**AMT**	**1966**	**300**	**165**	**90**

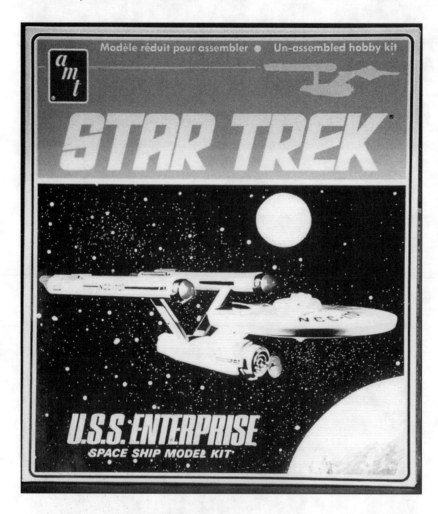

This model came in a lighted and unlighted version. The top price goes to the lighted version in a vertically designed box. The box art is effective, but there's room for improvement. (Beware, this and others were released three or four times over the years. Price pertains to original issue only.)

MODEL, KLINGON SHIP	**AMT**	**1966**	**400**	**220**	**120**

The Klingon ship also came lighted and unlighted, but the box was horizontal. Again, beware of reissues.

			Mint	Ex	Good
MODEL, SPOCK	**AMT**	1966	200	110	60

Nice diorama of Spock shooting at a vicious two-headed snake. (Hardly a worthy opponent considering the parade of aliens that visited the series.) Box art is colorful and interesting. Re-release came in a smaller box with the same art. Check for dates before buying.

MOVIE VIEWER	**Chemtoy**	1967	30	16	10

Three-inch red and black plastic viewer.

PENCIL SET	**Hasbro**	1967	100	55	30

This art set came with a collection of pencils, paints, and predrawn sketches for coloring in. The box art shows the Enterprise in flight with a close-up of Kirk and Spock in the bottom right corner.

PHASER GUN	**Remco**	1968	200	110	60

The Star Trek Phaser Gun was a flashlight with a color wheel inside. It was battery operated and made a buzzing noise when triggered. This ray gun was a staple in the Remco stable, kept alive by new packaging and stickers for one show after another.

			Mint	Ex	Good
PHASER RAY GUN	**Azrak-Hamway**	**1976**	**25**	**15**	**5**

Number 6369 was battery operated with use of one Penlite battery and was advertised as a "space flashlight." The phaser ray gun had "click action noise."

PUZZLES, JIGSAW	**Whitman**	**1978**	**30**	**20**	**10**

Nice artwork makes these a winner, but again they were late-comers in the game.

ROCKET PISTOL	**Remco**	**1968**	**300**	**165**	**90**

Remco dug into the closet and came up with this generic gun and helmet to repackage. The helmet has big bubble eyes, making it look like some kind of giant bug's head. The pistol was ten inches long and shot caps or rubber-tipped missiles. The pistol was also sold separately with a photo of Spock actually using the gun. (I wonder how much they paid him to do that.) The gun alone sells for $150.

			Mint	Ex	Good
TRACER GUN	**Rayline**	**1966**	**125**	**65**	**45**

A plastic pistol with colored plastic discs.

| **VIEW-MASTER (#BK057)** | **GAF** | **1968** | **12** | **10** | **—** |

The usual set of wheels depicting "The Omega Glory" episode.

| **WALKIE-TALKIES** | **Remco** | **1968** | **50** | **27** | **15** |

The Star Trek Astro Walkie-Talkies were two microphones connected with a plastic cord. If you yelled loud enough you could hear your friend up to twenty feet away. The set came shrink-wrapped on a card, no box.

LAND OF THE GIANTS

September 22, 1968 - September 6, 1970

Imagine a place where a cat is the size of a Tyrannosaurus, a drop of rain equals a flood, and a single slice of bread feeds twelve. Imagine *The Land of the Giants*. On second thought, you don't have to imagine—just feast your eyes on Irwin Allen's fourth hit in less than five years. Using a combination of enlarged props and bluescreen effects, Allen created a world that was unlike anything airing on TV at the time. It was the story of seven people stranded on a planet so like our own, but mammoth in proportion. Gary Conway played Steve Burton, captain of the ill-fated flight. He was accompanied by co-pilot Dan Erickson (Don Marshall) and flight attendant Betty Hamilton (Heather Young). The Spindrift, a sub-orbital spacecraft painted in Irwin orange, was on its way to London when it was pulled into the magnetic force of a giant space warp. Passengers on the Spindrift included engineer Mark Wilson (Don Matheson), jet-setter Valerie Scott (Deanna Lund), orphan-boy Barry Lockridge (Stefan Arngrim), and thief and con man Alexander Fitzhugh (Kurt Kasner). Oh, and don't forget Chipper, Barry's yapping dog.

Week after week, the "little people" would ban together in an effort to survive while trying to find a way back to Earth. Early episodes were especially eerie and suspenseful as the giants were portrayed as lumbering slow-witted creatures. In the pilot episode, Steve and Valerie are captured in a bug box and taped to a table, ready to be dissected by a giant scientist. Barry and Fitzhugh do battle with a giant cat and the entire group hides from an oversized mutt by finding sanctuary inside a discarded egg carton. As the show progressed, the giants took on a more realistic look. They moved and talked like people of Earth, presumably to allow for more interaction between the "little people" and the homeworlders. Another addition was Inspector Kobick of the Secret Police (Kevin Hagen of *Little House on the Prairie* fame). In about half a dozen episodes, Kobick led his force in a mad hunt for these enemies of the state. By the second season, *Giants* went the way of Allen's previous hits. We were soon introduced to a long line of episodes featuring alien civilizations and embarrassingly silly plot lines. In "Pay the Piper," *Lost in Space* alumnus Jonathan Harris put in a ridiculous performance as a crazed piper who entrances the little people with his magic music. In the category of hide-your-eyes-awful is "Giants and All That Jazz," an attempt at humor with down and out boxer Sugar Ray Robinson in the lead. But fans of the series, be not daunted. Early episodes such as "Ghost Town," "Weird World," and "The Bounty Hunter" are solid, exciting stories with fantastic special effects.

Of all Irwin Allen's hit sci-fi series, the *Land of the Giants* logo was on more toys than any of the others combined. In the first year of the series, Remco owned the license to the show. At the time, the toy company was known for its battery operated plastic toys like the Firebird 99 Dashboard and the Tiger Joe Tank. Rather than produce new TV show designs that might have limited shelf time, Remco chose to repackage generic toys from their existing line, adding *Land of the Giants* logos and fancy box art to create the "look" of a new toy. Thus, bizarre hybrids were developed, like the LOTG Space Sled, which was in reality Remco's Supercar with a paint job. In 1969, Hasbro became the chief marketer of *LOTG* toys. With less ambition behind them, or perhaps a sense of the show's impending cancellation, most of the Hasbro toys are carded dime store products like Frisbees and flashlights. To a collector, it is the tacky appearance of these Hasbro toys that make them even more valued than their big brothers at Remco.

Land of the Giants Collectibles

			Mint	Ex	Good
BAGATELLE GAME	Hasbro	1969	150	82	45

This is called the Land of the Giants Double Action Bagatelle Game. By the time you say it, the store's sold out. Actually, it's a plastic pinball type game with a cardboard back piece that features photos from the show.

BOOK	Pyramid Books	1968	—	7.50	—

The *Land of the Giants* paperback was a novel by Murray Leinster "based on the spectacular ABC-TV series created and produced by Irwin Allen."

			Mint	Ex	Good
COLORFORMS	**Colorforms**	**1968**	**125**	**70**	**40**

Boxed set of colorforms features a giant house setting with vinyl stick-ons of the show's characters, as well as their famous props, the giant safety pin and match hatchet. Nice box art.

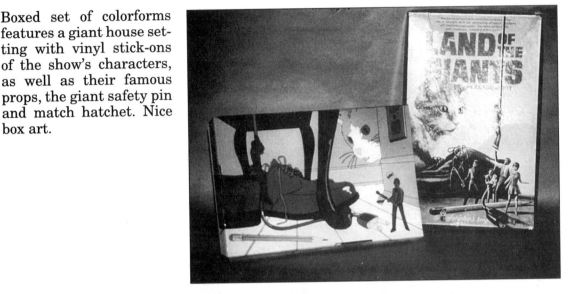

COLORING BOOK	**Whitman**	**1968**	**40**	**22**	**12**

Basic coloring book with an artwork cover. Nuff said.

COMIC BOOK	**Gold Key**	**1968**	**25**	**15**	**10**

Gold Key produced five issues of the *Giants* comics. Issue #5 is the hardest to find; expect to pay more. Issue #1 is pictured.

			Mint	Ex	Good
COSTUMES	**Ben Cooper**	1968	**150**	**82**	**45**

Ben Cooper produced three different costumes for Halloween. Steve Burton, Giant Witch (huh?), and Giant Scientist. All are polyester jumpsuits with plastic full face masks.

			Mint	Ex	Good
FLASHLIGHT	**Bantam Lite**	1968	**100**	**55**	**30**

Small flashlight that you could wear on your wrist. This came shrink-wrapped to a card and was probably featured on the Woolworth's checkout rack for around forty cents.

			Mint	Ex	Good
FLYING SAUCER	**Remco**	1968	**100**	**55**	**30**

One of Remco's easiest package switches, a Frisbee with an *LOTG* logo on it. Yes, people are actually paying $100 for a Frisbee.

			Mint	Ex	Good
GAME, BOARD	**Ideal**	1968	**150**	**82**	**45**

The game is pretty standard. Travel the board picking up items needed to repair the ship without getting caught by a giant. The box art features a giant cat attacking our heroes. Again, nice art, great color. Generally sells for more than most games of the era.

			Mint	Ex	Good
GUM CARDS	**Topps/A&BC**	1968	**700**	**385**	**210**

The debate still reigns on this short-lived series of bubble gum cards. The set of fifty-five cards was produced in the United States and in England. It is said that the English cards are smaller than their American cousins, but otherwise the same. Other experts claim that the set was only test marketed in the U.S., but was widely released in England, making them a highly coveted item. Either way, expect to pay upwards of $700 for a set, $150 and up for a wrapper or a display box.

			Mint	Ex	Good
LUNCH BOX	**Aladdin**	**1969**	**250**	**140**	**75**

This lunch box is highly collected by box collectors because it features a self portrait of famous Aladdin artist Elmer Lenhardt as the malevolent-looking giant scientist. The box is primarily green with a detailed action sequence on each side and cast sketches all around the edges.

MODEL, SNAKE	**Aurora**	**1968**	**1000**	**550**	**300**

This model kit features a giant snake about to take a bite out of Steve, Fitzhugh, and Betty. The box art is a classic piece of Aurora design work and is often sold alone or duplicated by laser printer. When buying, make sure it's the real thing before plunking down your money. An original sells for $1000. Repros can be bought for close to $200.

			Mint	Ex	Good
MODEL, SPINDRIFT	**Aurora**	**1968**	**1000**	**550**	**300**

The Spindrift was a double hit for Aurora. The original release featured an actual photo of the model laying under a large branch with a logo panel superimposed on the right side of the box. When *Giants* was canceled in 1970, Aurora redesigned the box to play up the "spaceship" angle and downplay the show. The 1975 box shows a sketch of the ship in flight with the words Rocket Transport Spindrift, followed by "from Land of the Giants" in very small print. 1968 sells for $700-$1000; 1975 model slightly less, $500-$750.

MOTORIZED FLYING ROCKET	**Remco**	**1968**	**150**	**82**	**45**

This toy was basically a plastic glider plane with a small motor and guide wires that you could manipulate to make the plane do tricks. Again, the box was more impressive than the toy, especially when you consider that it didn't resemble anything used on the actual show.

MOVIE VIEWER	**Acme**	**1968**	**60**	**33**	**18**

This cheap plastic viewer came on a photo backing card with two tiny rolls of film. The film wasn't even made with actual photos. They were hand-drawn scenes from the comic book with a silly story about a bird helping out the little people. (Acme? Aren't they the guys who sell to Wile E. Coyote?)

PAINTING SET	**Hasbro**	**1969**	**100**	**55**	**30**

Like its little brother the pencil set, this budding artist kit came with a row of oil paints and several canvas sketches.

PENCIL SET	**Hasbro**	**1969**	**100**	**55**	**30**

Twelve colored pencils with number coded pictures. Just make sure you color the Spindrift orange. (Make Irwin proud.)

			Mint	Ex	Good
PUZZLE, FLOOR	Whitman	1968	75	40	22

When put together, this round puzzle shows a sketch of Steve, Valerie, and Barry being menaced by that darn cat again.

RUB-ONS	Hasbro	1969	40	22	12

Remember Presto Magic Rub-Ons? A sheet of waxy paper with several images tattooed on the face. You lay your picture on the enclosed paper scene, rub with the back of the spoon and, voilà your image transfers to the paper. Cool, huh?

SIGNAL RAY SPACE GUN	Remco	1968	150	82	45

This revamp of the *Lost in Space* ray gun shot beams of colored lights (ooh, aah). You'll find it repackaged as the Star Trek Ray Gun in the same year. Again, go for the box.

SPACE SLED	Remco	1968	500	275	150

Those Remco geniuses took Gerry Anderson's Supercar and painted it to suit *Giants*. The car came with four directional discs that snapped to the underside to make the car drive in loops or figure eights. They didn't even bother to remove Supercar's star Mike Mercury from his seat behind the wheel. Again, there was nothing even close to this on the actual show, but who cares.

SPACESHIP CONTROL PANEL	Remco	1968	600	330	180

Remco's generic battery operated dashboard became the spaceship control panel with the addition of a few decals and a cardboard logo where the windshield ought to be. This toy was pricey for the sixties, selling for almost six dollars.

			Mint	Ex	Good
SPINDRIFT TOOTHPICK KIT	Remco	1968	125	70	40

Now this one takes the prize for cheap. It's a box full of toothpicks (yes, real wooden toothpicks) with a few cardboard shapes thrown in for shape. That's it. One hundred twenty-five dollars for a box of toothpicks. Now that's America for you.

TARGET RIFLE	Remco	1968	400	220	120

TARGET RIFLE (cont.)

Remco took their basic Western rifle and stuck an *LOTG* logo sticker on the stock to create this masterpiece. The Shoot and Stick Target Rifle included a target adorned with the logo, along with a supply of Velcro tipped darts. The box for this baby is lined with great phrases like "It's accurate … just like a real rifle," and "Professionally tested."

			Mint	Ex	Good
TARGET SET	**Hasbro**	**1969**	**75**	**40**	**22**

This set of suction cup darts came with a plastic gun and a logo target to aim at.

VIEW-MASTER (#B494)	**GAF**	**1968**	**65**	**55**	**—**

Basic View-Master wheels depicting the pilot episode entitled "The Crash." The photos are clearer and brighter than the actual episode since GAF used their own photographers to shoot on the set at the time.

WALKIE-TALKIES	**Remco**	**1968**	**150**	**82**	**45**

Basic walkie-talkies with stickers added, and you guessed it, a great box.

VOYAGE TO THE BOTTOM OF THE SEA

September 1964 - September 1968

Dive. Prepare to dive. Clear the decks. Secure all watertight hatches. We are about to take a voyage to the bottom of the sea. And you'll never believe what we find down there: giant octopods, alien spaceships, enemy labs, and lobster men that would like to see us humans served hot with melted butter. Weird? Hey, it's an Irwin Allen production. Hot on the heels of Irwin's smash movie of the same name, Twentieth Century Fox gave the producer his first shot at a TV series. It was about the crew of the futuristic nuclear sub Seaview. Veteran dramatic actor Richard Basehart was aboard as Admiral Harriman Nelson (played by Walter Pigeon in the film). David Hedison, who had made a name for himself as the scientist turned insect in *The Fly*, came aboard as Captain Lee Crane. While action and adventure made the series good boy toy fare, it was Hedison's dashing figure that sent females into a swooning faint. Scattered around the Seaview was a cast of background staples. Robert Dowdell (Chip Morton) came straight off the series *Stoney Burke*. Henry Kulky, who had played strong-man parts in the movies (notably Mighty Joe Young), played Curly, the ship's chief engineer for the first season. (I can't do it, captain, the engines'll blow.) (Oops, wrong chief engineer.) When Henry Kulky passed away suddenly, he was replaced by a younger, more comical chief, Sharkey, played by Terry Becker. To any TV addict of the era, Richard Bull, the Seaview's resident doctor, will be a familiar character actor with one of those faces you recognize but whose name you never know. Add to the mix a stellar cast of visitors like Robert Duvall, Michael Ansara, and Victor Buono and you've got one wowzer of a series. Well, at least for the first year or two.

The first season of *Voyage to the Bottom of Sea* was played as straight as you could get with a sci-fi series. Plots revolved around acts of political intrigue, assassinations, and government spies. The show was filmed in black and white and although the bad guys were never labeled, anti-Russian sentiments ran high. Look for stories written by Harlan Ellison and suspenseful shadowy directing by Sobey Martin and Leonard Horn. Set your VCR for "Long Live the King," a Christmas story that features Carroll O'Connor as a mysterious drifter who aids the men of the Seaview in their attempt to safeguard a small boy who is heir to his country's throne. This episode typifies the thoughtful plots of the first season, balancing the religious themes of Christmas with the political controversy of U.S. aid to foreign nations. Yes, I am talking about *Voyage to the Bottom of the Sea*. Just not the season most people remember. By the end of the third season, *Voyage* had changed into living color and with the color came a kaleidoscope of creatures. There was the Fossil Man, The Plant Man, The Shadowman, The Mummy, The Mermaid and The Man-Beast. By the end of the series' run, the crew of the Seaview had enough close encounters to fill the pages of *The National Inquirer* for years to come. Still, third and fourth season *Voyage* can be a hoot.

VCR ALERT: You have to check out "Deadly Dolls." Vincent Price makes a "priceless" appearance as a puppeteer whose puppets want to take over the Seaview for a maniacal purpose of their own. Watch for the Admiral Nelson puppet, which was crafted to an amazing likeness of Richard Basehart. If anybody finds one of those toys on the market today, it's worth all the gold in Davy Jones's Locker.

Voyage to the Bottom of the Sea Collectibles

			Mint	Ex	Good
BOOK	**Whitman**	**1965**	—	**5**	—

The spine states this is the "authorized TV adventure." Hardcover.

COLORING BOOK	**Whitman**	**1964**	**40**	**22**	**12**

Here's another oddity. The Whitman version of this coloring book has more pages and came complete with an official pack of crayons. The shorter version of the coloring book has the same cover but the name Watkins/Strathmore in the upper corner. Either way, the book contains an exciting original story about the rescue of a boy lost at sea. (Leftover Flipper plot, no doubt).

			Mint	Ex	Good
COMICS	**Dell/Gold Key**	**61-70**	**20**	**10**	**4**

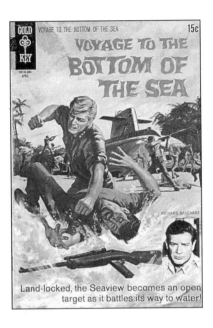

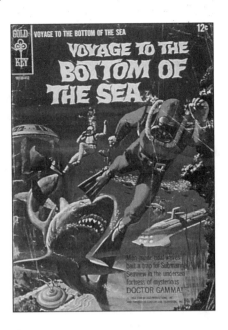

Set of sixteen comic books. Fifteen and sixteen are reprints. Artwork covers are fairly similar—giant octopus attacking the sub sort of thing.

			Mint	Ex	Good
FOUR-WAY SUB GUN	**Remco**	**1965**	**1,000**	**550**	**300**

This is a rare one. Taken from Remco's shelf of generic toys, this gun was designed to snap together to make four different weapons: a bazooka, a submarine gun, a Tommy gun, and a torpedo gun. "Converts Rapidly for Fun-Action" claims the box. Great, you can shoot your friends without wasting precious time. The gun itself was a spacey looking thing with a logo sticker on the handle. It was packaged with an extension and two rubber-tipped torpedoes.

			Mint	Ex	Good
GAME, BOARD	**Milton Bradley**	**1964**	**75**	**40**	**22**

The *Voyage* board game features artwork of a helicopter swooping down on Admiral Nelson's car (based on a scene from the pilot episode). It is odd to note that the Seaview is fairly hidden in the lower left-hand corner of the box. Again, the game is indicative of *Voyage*'s early season where political intrigue was hot. If the game had been produced later in the run, it surely would have featured a giant hairy creature eating the sub for lunch.

			Mint	Ex	Good
GAME, CARD	**Milton Bradley**	1964	60	33	18

"During their long undersea voyages, the crew of the SEAVIEW relaxes by playing card games. This is one of their favorites." So sayeth the instructions for this game. If you ask me, the men of the Seaview wouldn't be caught dead playing this souped up version of Old Maid. Match your sub cards by color or number. The first to give away all their cards wins. Somebody had better teach these guys poker.

			Mint	Ex	Good
GUM CARDS	**Donruss**	1964	100	55	30

Black and white set of sixty-six cards depicts mostly scenes from the series, such as card twelve ("War Conference") and card thirty-two ("Torpedoes Away"). The photos are nice and fairly clear. Each card has a paragraph of text on the back explaining the scene, and the tag line "Watch Voyage to the Bottom of the Sea on Your Local ABC Station" Although the cards say "Series 1" on them, there never was a Series 2. What a shame. Color shots of the Lobster Man would have been way cool. Expect to pay upwards of $50 for the box or a wrapper.

			Mint	Ex	Good
LUNCH BOX	**Aladdin**	**1967**	**125**	**70**	**40**

Although Aladdin is generally known for great artwork, this box doesn't make the grade. The colors are fine, the Seaview is great, and the character likenesses are well done. Unfortunately, there is a huge, bug-eyed, silly looking red octopus on EVERY side of the box. You can't escape him, no matter which way you turn the box. The artist was obviously watching third season episodes when he designed this one. Still, in all, you can't beat a good old metal lunch box, even one as silly as this.

MODEL, FLYING SUB	**Aurora**	**1968**	**500**	**275**	**150**
		1975	**200**	**110**	**60**

This was one of Aurora's more detailed kits. The interior of the sub was highly detailed with tiny control panels and Lee Crane in the pilot's seat. It was molded in yellow and the small interior was a painter's nightmare (especially when you're only ten). Original cost: $1.50. This model was reissued in 1975 under the Monogram Models label. It is identical to its big brother, but the box art is a bit more sophisticated with digital lettering as a sign of the times.

91   The Final Frontier

			Mint	Ex	Good
MODEL, SEAVIEW	Aurora	1966	500	275	150
		1975	200	110	60

This classic Aurora kit was an easy build. The model itself is nothing special, but Aurora art collectors will pay top dollar for the empty box. The box art depicts the Seaview underwater moving toward the right. Original price: $1.00. Like many of the Aurora kits, this one was reissued in 1975. Since *Voyage* was off the air, Aurora changed the wording on the box to "Nuclear Submarine Seaview" in big letters with the show's name in small print underneath. The reissue box has the sub moving toward the left and it is done in much lighter colors. **Check out Lunar Models for newly cast versions of the Seaview and the Flying Sub. Tough to build, but excellent quality.

			Mint	Ex	Good
PLAY SETS	Remco	1965	150	82	45

Well planned packaging made this toy a good seller on the shelves of Sears in 1965. Two different play sets were offered in a package that looked like an underwater diorama. The front of the box was cut out and covered in plastic so shoppers could easily view the toy inside. The Seascout set came with a yellow plastic mini sled and a yellow sea crawler. The Seaview set came with an eighteen-inch plastic Seaview that was powered by rubber band. The set also included several figures and an octopus to create your own underwater havoc.

			Mint	Ex	Good
PUZZLES, FLOOR	Whitman	1964	50	27	15

Whitman, the children's book publisher, released several different puzzles as part of their Jr. Jigsaw series. These were 100-piece floor puzzles with coloring book style pictures.

			Mint	Ex	Good
PUZZLES, TRAY	**Milton Bradley**	**1964**	**50**	**27**	**15**

MB didn't stop with just games. They designed a series of frame style puzzles with artwork that was more sophisticated than Whitman's. MB's puzzles were "Aptitude Tested Puzzles for ages 4-9." (How reassuring for parents.)

VIEW-MASTER (#B483)/ TRU-VUE	**GAF**	**66/68**	**12**	**10**	**—**

Both sets of 3-D slides depict scenes from "Deadly Creature Below." As with all View-Master wheels, the photos are clear and detailed. The Tru-Vue slides were rectangular and made to fit a larger viewer.

DARK SHADOWS

June 1966 - April 1971

An old Gothic mansion sits on the edge of a cliff. A barrage of wind-tossed waves batters the cliff as a woman's voice rises above the music ... "My name is Victoria Winters ...." And so begins a journey into fantasy, horror, and gothic style romance. A place called Collinwood where vampires hide, werewolves lurk, and the odd zombie comes out to play every now and again. You are in a place full of *Dark Shadows*.

In 1966, Dan Curtis had a revolutionary idea for daytime TV. In a tube populated with the likes of *As the World Turns* and *Secret Storm*, Curtis wanted something different, something that tapped into the old spooky romance novels that women read like kids read comic books. *Dark Shadows* didn't start out to be horror based. The original plot surrounded an orphan girl named Victoria Winters (played by Alexandra Moltke) who comes to a small New England town to act as governess to a young boy. There she becomes involved with the odd members of the Collins family. Elizabeth, played by veteran movie actress Joan Bennett, was the senior lady of the house, a recluse with secrets involving her husband's death. Her brother Roger, played as despicably as possible by Louis Edmonds (now of *All My Children* fame), is at his very best a drunken leech. Roger's boy David (David Henesey) is born trouble, while Elizabeth's daughter Carolyn (Nancy Barrett) has her own reputation in town. *Dark Shadows* had all the makings of your average everyday soap opera until cousin Barnabas came to visit. The day Jonathan Frid put in his first pair of fangs, *Dark Shadows* took a turn in a whole new direction. Their audience grew by leaps and bounds. Now not only were housewives watching, but so were college kids and teens running home from Jr. High. Even more baffling than the high ratings was the sex appeal of a 200-year-old vampire. Actor Jonathan Frid was bombarded with love letters from women dying to have him sink his teeth into them. Once the skeletons were let out of the closet, so to speak, *Dark Shadows* began its dance with the encyclopedia of the supernatural. Angelique (Lara Parker) joined the cast as the beautiful and tantalizing witch who had cursed Barnabas with the kiss of the vampire. Kate Jackson of *Charlie's Angels* fame made her first TV appearance as a ghost, later to become one of the series' featured players. Grayson Hall, a moody looking lady with a deep throaty voice, became Dr. Julia Hoffman, a sort of mad scientist set on freeing Barnabas from his undead state. Actually, Julia became somewhat of a love interest for Barnabas and with her appearances, she softened the character until he became one of the good guys. Minus their famous villain, Curtis brought in David Selby as Quentin Collins, resident werewolf and all-around nasty fellow, to fill the bill. Pure evil incarnate, Selby's fan mail soon equaled that of Frid. It was a daytime phenomenon.

When Curtis finally put the series to bed in 1971, there were two movies in the making, a series of twenty-some paperbacks, a record album, and a whole collection of toys all bearing the name of *Dark Shadows*. Then something unprecedented happened. This daytime drama became the first soap opera to be sold into syndication and eventually put on video tape for sale at the local movie store. Fans of *Dark Shadows* still hold yearly pilgrimages to the Collinwood set in New York. New fan magazines, t-shirts, and photos still show up from time to time and Jonathan Frid still gets asked for his autograph. With all of this public attention, it's hard to imagine the series has been off the air for over twenty years. But like the ghosts of Collinwood, it seems that *Dark Shadows* is destined to go on haunting us for years to come.

Dark Shadows Collectibles

		Mint	Ex	Good
BOOKS, PAPERBACK	**Dell**	**15**	**8**	**5**

While not toys, no DS collector would be caught "un-dead" without his own set of DS paperbacks. These novels, with their familiar gold bindings, were all written under the name Marilyn Ross. The first several books were released with sketched covers, but those were soon re-released with photo covers from the show. The first ten or twelve books follow the series fairly closely, but then the Barnabas and Quentin series of books came about with wild story lines like aliens invading Collinwood. The books were marvelous sellers in the late sixties, retailing for seventy-five cents then up to $1.25, with a new adventure coming out almost every two weeks for awhile. (I wrote every one of my sixth grade book reports on those novels, much to my teacher's dismay.) Also look for Barnabas Collins in a *Very Funny Vein*, which is a joke book. I do believe there's a cookbook out there too. Haunt your local secondhand bookstore; these guys are regulars.

			Mint	Ex	Good
COMICS	**Gold Key**	**69-76**	**40**	**15**	**6**

Gold Key produced thirty-five issues of the DS comic books with the help of Dan Curtis Productions. Issues 1-5 came with a pull-out poster. All had pretty tame story lines considering what horror comics of the time were like (ever read Tales of the Crypt?). Graphics were okay. For the young teen audience they were aimed at, they were spooky enough.
**Also look for miniature comic books based on DS and other shows. These were made by Western Publishing as giveaways to promote the comics. The books are only about 2" x 6", stapled in the middle, no covers.

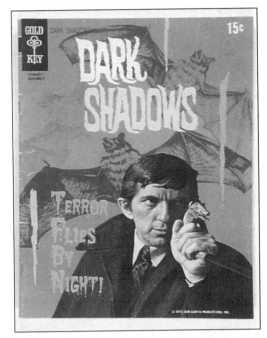

GAME, BARNABAS COLLINS	**Milton Bradley**	**1969**	**60**	**33**	**18**

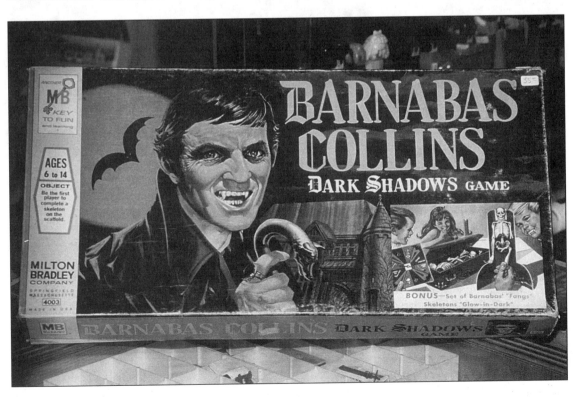

GAME, BARNABAS COLLINS (cont.)

This game was a boon for anatomy classes. The object was to build your own skeleton on a hangman's scaffold before the other players do. Collect one rib cage, one head, four parts to the arms, four parts to the legs ("the thigh bone's connected to the hip bone, the leg bone's connected to the thigh bone"—sing along now). The game came with a cardboard coffin with a plastic lid (one cheap version and one nicer one, depending on which release of the game you bought), a whole parcel of plastic bones, four cardboard scaffolds, and your own set of vampire fangs. Great gruesome fun. Look for a nice character sketch of Barnabas on the box lid.

		Mint	Ex	Good
GAME, DARK SHADOWS Whitman	1968	75	40	22

This game was a little more traditional. It consisted of a basic playing board imprinted on heavy paper and cardboard movers with a stack of cards to tell you how to move. The game is filled with cutesy graphics of tombstones, black cats, and bats. The box lid has a sketch of a generic looking vampire with the *Dark Shadows* logo and a small shot of the Collinwood house. Of the two games, this one is generally harder to find.

GUM CARDS	Philly Gum	1968	150	82	45

Don't get confused by this one. Philly Gum made two different series of cards but labeled them both 1-66. Referred to by *DS* aficionados as the "Pink Set" and the "Green Set" because one set has a green border and one has a pink border, natch. The pink set came out first. The wrapper and box both featured a photo of Barnabas Collins with the words "TV's Cool Ghoul Barnabas." There are no captions on the cards and the backs fit together to make a puzzle. Many of the pink cards were "autographed" by Barnabas and friends with authentic looking signatures. The green set uses a photo of the Collins's house with the *Dark Shadows* logo on the wrapper and box. This set has lines from the series as captions printed in a garish pink box on the front of each card. The sets are equally valued, as are the wrappers and boxes, which sell for $20-$50 on a wrapper, $75-$100 on the box.

			Mint	**Ex**	**Good**
JOSETTE'S MUSIC BOX	Dan Curtis	1970	450	250	135

When I was thirteen, this is the thing I wanted most in life. Advertised in the back of *Famous Monsters*, the music box appeared to be made of gold and glass, a replica of the precious antique on *DS*. It was way out of my allowance range. Today, it's still out of my allowance range, but the gild is off the lily. Josette's music box is a plastic cylinder with a plastic lid painted copper. It does play Quentin's theme when wound and it is labeled on the inside. It came in a cardboard box with Barnabas's picture on the front. Come to think of it, cheap quality or not, I still have cravings for this one.

MODEL, BARNABAS	**MPC**	1968	250	140	75

When built, this kit made a rather menacing looking figure of Barnabas Collins in his famous Inverness coat with his wolf's head cane. Nice likeness of the actor and good detail makes this a nice find. The box is good, but it would be a shame not to build this one.

MODEL, BARNABAS VAMPIRE VAN	**MPC**	1969	150	82	45

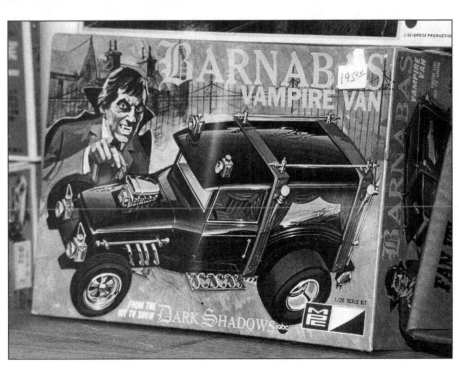

MODEL, BARNABAS VAMPIRE VAN (cont.)

This is another example of great model making from the sixties. The van is actually a hearse with dragster modifications. The model itself is really nothing special since it resembles most generic dragster models of the era, but the nice box graphics of a vicious looking Barnabas behind a close-up of the car make it collectible. As with all models, prices are for unassembled kit still in the box.

			Mint	Ex	Good
PILLOWS, HORROR HEAD	Centsable	1969	100	55	30

In what has to be a rip-off of a license, Centsable produced three stuffed heads painted with fluorescent colors. The Witch, Vampire, and Werewolf all came in individual boxes with the *Dark Shadows* logo.

PINUPS, GIANT	**Philly Gum**	**1969**	10	6	3

Philly Gum was determined to make good use of the license while they had it. In 1969 they released a set of pinup posters that came folded inside of a waxy wrapper like the gum cards. There were sixteen different posters from the show done in black and white with those same green and pink colors used in the frames and lettering. Although most of the posters featured well-known characters from the series, like Barnabas, Quentin, and Angelique, they also went a little off with photos of Evon Hanley and Jamison Collins. Who? Got me. Guess we'll have to find a really die-hard fan for the answer to that one.

			Mint	Ex	Good
VIEW-MASTER (#B503)	**GAF**	**1968**	**75**	**64**	—

The usual round wheels with photos from the show. Nice photo cover makes it a good find.

THE OUTER LIMITS

September 1963 - January 1965

"The mind of man has always longed to know what lies beyond the world we live in. Explorers have ventured into the depths and the heights. Of these explorers, some are scientists, some are mystics. Each is driven by a different purpose. The one thing they share in common is a wish to cross the borderlands that lie beyond the Outer Limits."

So sayeth the Control Voice. You remember him, that mysterious, detached voice that opened and closed each show. Was he a man? A machine? Or perhaps an alien looking down on us in wonder? If you did ever wonder, then producer Joseph Stefano did his job well.

The Outer Limits was created by Leslie Clark Stevens for fledgling production studio Daystar. He wanted to make a science fiction show, but with real science. Not Buck Rogers style with ray guns and evil aliens attempting to take over the world. Every episode of the series had to start with a science fact, then extrapolate on the theme. Start with robots, then jump to the question of robotic rights when one is put on trial for murder ("I Robot"). Take an innocent laser device that becomes a gateway for an alien to enter our dimension ("The Bellero Shield"). And what happens when the first astronaut to visit Venus starts mutating before our eyes ("Cold Hands, Warm Heart")? (Remember the one about the vicious doll, Talking Tina? Oh, no that was a *Twilight Zone*. Never mind.) From its very first episode entitled "The Galaxy Being," *The Outer Limits* gave us an incredible list of talented guest stars such as Cliff Robertson, David McCallum, Martin Landau, Martin Sheen, Sally Kellerman, William Shatner, Leonard Nimoy, Robert Culp, Carol O'Connor, and Donald Pleasance. Even more memorable were the creatures, or BEARS, as Stefano liked to call them. The ants with the beatnik faces known as "The Zanti Misfits," The Thetan from "Architects of Fear," the Ebonite Interrogator from "Nightmare," and don't forget the "'It' [that] Crawled out of the Woodwork." With its technological base and dialogue that kept you running for your dictionary, it's a wonder the show was licensed to toy manufacturers at all. But as toy manufacturers will, they latched onto the monster aspect of the show, creating toys more suited to the Creature Double Feature than a sophisticated sci-fi series like *The Outer Limits*.

All right, you didn't think I'd stop without doing it. I give in, here goes. "There is nothing wrong with your television set. Do not attempt to adjust the picture. We will control the horizontal. We will control the vertical. We can change the focus to a soft blur or sharpen it to crystal clarity. For the next hour sit quietly and we will control all that you see and hear. You are about to participate in a great adventure. You are about to experience the awe and mystery which reaches from the inner mind to … THE OUTER LIMITS!!!!!!!!

The Outer Limits Collectibles

			Mint	Ex	Good
COMICS	**Dell**	**1964-69**	**15**	**7**	**3**

In the true spirit of comics with an educational base, Dell produced *The Outer Limits* comics. Unfortunately, most of the issues deal with the "aliens have come to take over Earth" theme, again ignoring Stefano's interest in presenting real science. Issues are numbered 1-18, but 17 and 18 are reissues of 1 and 2 that were released in 1969. Originally selling for twelve cents each, the first ten issues sell for $5-$15, later issues under $5.

COSTUME	**Collegeville**	**1964**	**250**	**140**	**75**

Standard polyester jumpsuit with monsters on the front and a monster mask. (Imagine a six-year-old asking for an *Outer Limits* costume for Halloween? Couldn't have been a very big seller.) Pretty rare piece.

			Mint	Ex	Good
GAME, BOARD	**Milton Bradley**	1964	250	140	75

Like the series, this game took the basic roll-the-dice-board-game one step further. The board is divided into four "Tracking Labs" with a monster invading each. Players must collect all four parts of their monster, then destroy him, to win the game. The box art depicts three *Limits* monsters heading our way in front of a funky alien-looking landscape.

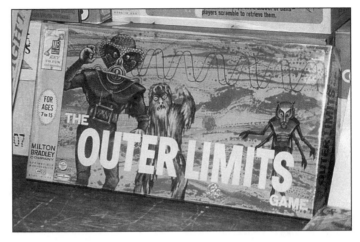

GUM CARDS	**Bubbles, Inc.**	1964	300	165	90

Set of fifty cards were produced in color, although admittedly garish colors. Each depicts a scene from the series with description on the back. As with the other toys, emphasis was on the monsters from the series, with scary one-liners on the cards like, "You are in my power" and "Living Nightmare." Wrapper: $60-$80, box: $400-$500. And by the way, Bubbles, Inc.? Do any of you South Philadelphians remember Dr. Shock? What do you think?

MODEL KIT	**Golden Era Models, Inc.**	—	50	—

The Sixth Finger Model Kit contained one figure (obviously with twelve fingers), a base, and of course, a nasty-looking vial of who-knows-what.

			Mint	Ex	Good
MODELS	**Lunar Models**	**1990s**	**125**	**70**	**40**

Although not a collectible of the era, fans of the show will want to check out Lunar Models in Texas. They are in the process of releasing models based on the show's most famous monsters. All of their models are extremely detailed and not for the beginner hobbyist, but when built, they are fantastic representations of the episodes that have made the series popular. Models vary in price from $80-$125, but have no real resale value.

			Mint	Ex	Good
PUZZLES, JIGSAW	**Milton Bradley**	**1964**	**150**	**82**	**45**

These 100-piece 19" x 20-1/2" boxed puzzles came in an 8" x 13" box with nice graphics from the show on each side. There seem to be at least six different puzzles, each based on a different episode. Milton Bradley also made "Junior" jigsaw puzzles (10-1/8" x 19") designed for pre-teens.

THE FIRST FRONTIER:

WESTERNS ON TELEVISION

There was a time when every boy under ten owned an imitation leather holster and a pair of shiny metal cap pistols. Even the girls in the neighborhood had their fake buckskin skirts and cowgirl boots. Western was in. Children of both sexes were glued to their TV sets to watch Lucas McCain save his son from cattle rustlers, or Marshall Matt Dillon ride the bad guys out on a rail. And what American family would miss Sunday nights with the Cartwrights? Westerns of the late fifties and early sixties gave the viewers a sense of right and wrong, black and white, truth against lies. In Virginia City or Dodge, one man could make a difference and fighting for your beliefs was an admirable thing to do. The plots were simple, well suited for family viewing. There was a lot of shooting but very little bloodshed, and moral values ran high.

The trappings of a TV cowboy made for long lines at the local toy store. Cap pistols, suction cup rifles, cowboy and Indian costumes, bows and arrows, ride-on horses and chuck wagon gear—the choices were endless. In 1966, American Character made a name in the toy biz by releasing a set of Bonanza action figures (read "dolls" for boys). The set was designed to encourage accessory sales of items such as horses, wagons, and a villain or two to add drama. Toy dealers were not overly enthused about the idea at the time, but detailed display units (a highly sought after collectible) and a well-timed TV commercial campaign made the toys a winner for dealers and American Character. When it came to Western marketing, the toy gun was the answer to large profits. In direct contrast to today's standards, buying your child a set of six shooters was the cool thing to do. Commercials of the era showed children happily killing their friends with the latest in retro-weaponry. Cap guns were manufactured in dozens of forms, from pistols to rifles, and don't forget Johnny Reb, the toy cannon that actually worked. In the nineties, the thought of stocking a toy cannon on the shelves of Toys R Us is as unlikely as stocking a toy guillotine. With all the joy and pleasure we associated with playing cowboy, it was Alfred Hitchcock who truly took a long look at what society was condoning. In his series episode entitled "Bang, You're Dead," a five-year-old Billy Mumy gallops all over town playing cowboy with what is actually a real loaded handgun. The audience is treated to a half hour of breath-holding suspense as the little boy aims his gun at various innocent bystanders he meets along the way. Hitchcock made his point about the dangers of "toy" guns—a point that has certainly taken root in the nineties.

However, putting all the moralizing and psychiatry aside, what could be better than riding the range on your pinto pony, your collie at your side and a rib dinner waiting at the end of the trail? When you think cowboy, think of sleeping beneath a star-filled sky, the smell of a freshly cut pine, the relief of sinking into a hot tub after a long day in the sun, square dances, box lunches, and homemade apple pie. Kind of beats nine to five and the freeway, doesn't it? To quote Willie Nelson, "My heroes have always been cowboys."

DANIEL BOONE

September 1964 - August 1970

Daniel Boone was a man, yes, a big man. With an eye like an eagle and as tall as a mountain was he. Kind of poetic, ain't it? Fess Parker joined the cast of NBC's new family series *Daniel Boone* after making a career as Davy Crockett for Disney. Although the series is not well remembered by most, it featured a sterling cast against a backdrop of beautiful scenery. Lounge singer Ed Ames played Boone's Indian friend Mingo. (Back in those days there wasn't an Indian on TV being played by an actual American Indian.) Albert Salmi co-starred as Yadkin. Patricia Blair (from *Rifleman* fame) played Boone's wife Rebecca, the patient good woman who was always left behind with the kids while her husband went off in search of adventure. Boone's daughter Jemima was played by Veronica Cartwright, sister to Angela of *Lost In Space* fame. Son Israel was played by white-haired youngster Darby Hinton. Hinton became an immediate teen idol, making the cover of *16* magazine. Semi-regulars included football great and needlepoint connoisseur Rosie Greer as Gabe Cooper, the runaway slave. The sausage man himself, Jimmy Dean, appeared as Josh Clements, a fur trapping friend of Boone's.

The story was supposed to be based on the actual life of pioneer Daniel Boone during the years preceding the Revolutionary War. The plots were full of Indian fights, but don't expect a lot of bloodshed. The show aired at 7:30 p.m. and kept a wholesome profile at all times. The best stories on the show were the simplest. Like *Little House on the Prairie, Daniel Boone* did a good job of representing the pioneer spirit—trapping and growing their own food, making their own clothes, warding off the ravages of the weather, pulling together to survive.

It may not be the biggest cult hit, but this little unassuming show did one thing that most shows would die for: it stayed in one time slot for six straight years. It aired against *The Munsters*. It aired against *Batman*. But the ratings never wavered. In 1966, *Daniel Boone* became a rather unusual lead-in for a new science fiction series named *Star Trek*. When *Trek* went off the air in 1969, Daniel Boone and company plugged on for another year. Who says a family show can't make it? This one really did.

Now for your reading pleasure, the rest of the song: "Daniel Boone was a man, yes, a big man. He was brave, he was fearless, and as tough as a mighty oak tree. From the coonskin cap on the top of old Dan to the tip of his rawhide boots, the rippin'est roarin'est fightin'est man the frontier ever knew. Daniel Boone was a man, yes, a big man. What a boon, what a doer, what a dream come a truer was he."

When it comes to collectibles, you'll notice Parker got himself a better agent this time around. To distinguish the toys from the old Disney version of *Daniel Boone*, all of the show's toys were labeled with Fess Parker's name before the name of the show.

Daniel Boone Collectibles

			Mint	Ex	Good
COLORING BOOK	**Saalfield**	**1964**	**30**	**17**	**9**

Actually called The Fess Parker Coloring Book, the sketch of Fess in buckskins and coonskin cap kind of tells it all.

FIGURE, DANIEL BOONE	**Remco**	**1964**	**160**	**75**	**35**

This figure of Boone was five inches tall and had a hard plastic body and a vinyl head. It came with a cloth coonskin cap and a long rifle.

GAME, BOARD	**Milton Bradley**	**1964**	**40**	**22**	**12**

The Fess Parker Trail Blazers 20" x 10" boxed game was subtitled "from the Daniel Boone TV Show." (It would seem Fess had a better agent than Daniel did.) Charming graphics show Boone whacking the heck out of two Indians with his rifle. I guess it was more wholesome than shooting them. The game came with your very own membership application to join the Trail Blazers Club at NBC.

LUNCH BOX	**King Seeley**	**1965**	**80**	**45**	**25**

Nick Lo Bianco took the old Fess Parker Davey Crockett box and reworked it to make the Fess Parker Daniel Boone steel lunch box. The artwork is nice, showing Boone in his buckskins preparing to fight the Indians.

LUNCH BOX	**SPP**	**1965**	**100**	**55**	**30**

This is a vinyl lunch box molded in tan with a sketch of Boone on the front. Believe it or not, the writing on the box says, "Fess Parker Kaboodle Kit from the Daniel Boone TV Show." There was no thermos. Apparently it was meant to carry kaboodles, not lunch.

			Mint	Ex	Good
PAINT SET	**Standard Toykraft**	1964	**80**	**45**	**25**

The Fess Parker Oil Paint-by-Number and Pencil-by-Number Set featured numbered drawings that you could paint or color of Fess as good old Daniel Boone. Undoubtedly an attempt to bring art to boys. Bet it wasn't a hot seller.

			Mint	Ex	Good
PLAY SET	**MPC**	1964	**200**	**110**	**60**

The (you guessed it) "Fess Parker as Daniel Boone from the Daniel Boone TV Series Frontier Attack" set. I kid you not, that's actually printed on the box. Like the Marx set, this was a box full of generic Western figures and accessories and was sold exclusively at Grant's department store.

			Mint	Ex	Good
PLAY SET	**Marx**	19??	**200**	**110**	**60**

Oh, those clever folks at Marx did it again. They packed up one of their old cowboys and Indians sets and threw it in a box with a sketch of Daniel Boone on the cover. Tadaaa, licensed merchandise without the risk. Actually, this set was probably produced as part of their generic western line and had no licensing link to the series. (If it had, it surely would have had Fess Parker's name emblazoned on it.)

			Mint	Ex	Good
VIEW-MASTER (#B479)	**GAF**	1964	**15**	**13**	**5**

You know what this is. I just thought I'd tell you it's out there.

BONANZA

September 1959 - January 1973

Think Virginia City, silver mining and tall timber. Think of one man raising three sons alone. Think Ponderosa. It's *Bonanza*, one of the most successful television shows ever made. Sunday night was *Bonanza* night. It aired on NBC at 9:00 p.m. for eleven years and was a staple in most American homes. From first episode to last, Lorne Greene always turned in a perfect performance as Ben Cartwright. He managed to play a tough, hard-nosed father who at the same time was an understanding, loving dad. His three sons, all born of different mothers, were as different as could be. Adam (Pernell Roberts) was the oldest. He was the son of Ben's first wife Elizabeth, from when Ben ran a ship's shop in New England. Well-educated, well-mannered, Adam was the businessman of the bunch, always serious with no time for play. Hoss (Dan Blocker) was a bear of a man. He was the son of Inga, a Swedish beauty killed by Indians while taking a wagon west. What Hoss lacked in schooling he made up for in sincerity. Little Joe (Michael Landon) was the youngest, the wildest, the dreamer in the bunch. He was the son of Ben's last wife, Marie, a playgirl in old New Orleans who was killed by a fall from a horse. Little Joe played hard and fell hard, never quite learning from his mistakes.

These characters created a family that Americans dreamed of belonging to. The kind of family that pulled together despite their differences. The kind that made it to the top with hard work and honesty. The men of *Bonanza* were heroes who boys could look up to (and they kept us girls watching too). *Bonanza* was a people show, not your typical shoot-'em-up Western. Actually, the gunplay was kept to a minimum in favor of a peaceful solution, or if all else failed, a good old-fashioned fistfight. Like an anthology series, *Bonanza* rotated the main characters, giving each one his own episode once a month, with an occasional ensemble show thrown in for good measure. Although *Bonanza* is categorized as a drama, some of their best episodes are comedy all the way. Like "The Hayburner," an episode in which Joe and Hoss are duped into buying a racehorse that couldn't win against a pack of snails. On the serious side, there are strong stories about a father dealing with growing old, about prejudice in the form of white man against red, and about the horror of vigilantism.

As the years passed, the faces began to change. Pernell Roberts was the first to go in a dispute over his desires to do more on the series. In his place came David Canary (now the star of *All My Children*) as ranch hand Candy. Redheaded, freckle-faced child actor Mitch Vogel joined the group in 1970 as Jamie Hunter, an orphan who was taken in by the Cartwrights. Then, most tragically, in 1972 Dan Blocker passed away unexpectedly, and *Bonanza* would never be the same. In its last year, the ratings dropped and the show began to struggle. Private eye shows had taken over for Westerns, with the highly rated *Hawaii Five-O* beating *Bonanza* in its time slot week after week. The Ponderosa had trouble moving into the 1900s just as *Bonanza* had trouble moving into the 1970s.

As you can imagine, licensing *Bonanza* was like striking the mother lode for toy companies. It was a natural. Cowboy toys had always been popular, with Roy Rogers and *Rifleman* paving the way. The American Character company struck it rich with their idea for a series of action figures based on the characters. (Yes, dolls for boys.) The figures and their horses and accessories are some of the most collectible pieces from the days of the Ponderosa.

Bonanza Collectibles

			Mint	Ex	Good
COLORING BOOK	**Saalfield**	**1965**	**25**	**14**	**8**

Two different versions were produced. One has a sketch of all four Cartwrights on the cover, while the other is missing Adam (a premonition perhaps?). Nice sketches and fairly cheap since there seemed to be thousands of them out there.

COMICS	**Dell/Gold Key**	**1960-70**	**30**	**15**	**5**

Dell produced thirty-seven comics in this set, but only a few have photo covers. Still, a Dell TV comic is always worth the read.

FIGURES, W/HORSE	**American Character 1966**	**200**	**110**	**60**
FIGURES, W/O HORSE		**100**	**55**	**30**

These hard plastic figures were eight inches tall and came packaged with or without a horse. Each set came with lots of small accessories like guns, canteens, ropes—all the basic cowboy paraphernalia. It is rumored that an Adam doll was made, but when Roberts left the series, the toy company painted on a mustache and sold him as the bad guy. Even stranger is the inscription that graces the bottom of every box just under the character's name: "FULL ACTION MAN." I think I'll have to check these guys out more closely.

	Mint	Ex	Good

GAME, RUMMY   **Parker Bros.**   **1964**   **50**   **27**   **15**

This was a cheap deal for Parker Bros. They took a plain old Michigan Rummy board and put it in a box with a photo of the Cartwrights playing cards on the lid. Ta-daaa, Bonanza Rummy. What will they think of next?

GUN AND HOLSTER   **Halpern Co.**   **1965**   **125**   **70**   **40**

The *Bonanza* logo is etched into the side of this simulated leather holster and gun belt. The belt came equipped with a pair of silver cap guns bearing the *Bonanza* logo.

GUNS OUTFIT   **Marx**   **1960s**   **225**   **145**   **75**

Included a twenty-five-inch cap firing saddle rifle with a magazine that pulled down to load, and a nine-and-one-half-inch Western pistol that fired two-piece Marx shooting bullets. The guns had wood-colored plastic stocks and gray plastic barrels. Came with a tan vinyl holster.

| LUNCH BOX | Aladdin | 1963 | 125 | 70 | 40 |

The first *Bonanza* lunch box showed all four Cartwrights riding the range and is primarily green. Art by Elmer Lenhardt.

| LUNCH BOX | Aladdin | 1965 | 75 | 40 | 22 |

Adam still makes an appearance on box number two, which is trimmed in brown. This one shows the Cartwrights in the street, standing ready to protect Virginia City. Elmer Lenhardt lent his pen for this one too.

| LUNCH BOX | Aladdin | 1968 | 75 | 40 | 22 |

This yellow lunch box was designed by, you guessed it, Elmer Lenhardt. The front shows a very accurate portrait of the family (sans Adam) riding with guns drawn. The box band shows an Indian attack in progress. The thermos for this one is particularly strange since it shows our heroes tied to a stake by the Indians. I guess Elmer was in a bad mood that week.

| MAGIC EYES SET | GAF | 1964 | 30 | 17 | 9 |

Basically a View-Master set, but instead of having round cards, it has rectangular cards made to fit a Tru-Vue Magic Eyes Set.

| MODEL | Revell | 1966 | 175 | 100 | 55 |

This big square box looks more like a board game than a model. The box art is a photo of Hoss, Ben and Little Joe encircled by a giant lariat. The model itself was a simple snap-together set that created three nine-inch figures when finished. Fairly rare, especially since figures were generally not a big seller.

PUZZLE, JIGSAW	Milton Bradley	1964	40	22	12

125-piece puzzle in a small box. Sketch is of Joe firing at a bad guy with his family riding in to help from behind. Came with a free poster included in the box.

RECORD ALBUM	RCA Victor	1964	—	20	8

Lorne Greene recorded this album titled "Welcome to the Ponderosa." It featured the big hit song, "Ringo."

VIEW-MASTER	GAF	1964	25	20	—

The usual: View-Master reels with nice photos. Always worth the price. I know of three reels, B471, BB497, and B487.

WAGON	American Character	1965	100

The Bonanza Four-in-One Wagon was made to accompany the American Character figures. The wagon came with dozens of accessories that made the vehicle interchangeable as a chuck wagon, an ore wagon, a ranch wagon, or a covered wagon. It includes two horses with "action hooves." The box has the *Bonanza* name but no pictures of the characters.

GUNSMOKE

September 1955 - September 1975

It is amazing to find that one of the longest running series on nighttime TV was a Western. You know, cowboys and Indians. The ones that went out of vogue in the sixties. Well, somehow Gunsmoke managed to hang on through three decades of television changes. The series actually started as a radio program with William Conrad (TV's Cannon) as the voice of Marshal Matt Dillon. In the mid-fifties CBS was keen on producing an "adult Western" as opposed to shows like *Roy Rogers* and *Rin Tin Tin* that were popular at the time. They settled on the radio show and had big plans for the lead. They wanted John Wayne to play Dillon. Unfortunately for them, the Duke didn't want to do a regular series, but suggested an unknown named James Arness (brother of *Mission: Impossible* star Peter Graves). Arness had made his acting debut as the Thing in the movie of the same name. It was his great height and all-around size that made him perfect for the monster and darn good for the role of the Dodge City Marshal. Alongside Arness was Milburn Stone as Doc Adams. They became the only two actors to last for the full run of the series. To give the show a softer side, Amanda Blake was cast as Kitty Russell, the owner of the Longbranch Saloon. Blake didn't play a femme fatale like many Western women did. She was tough—an independent woman who could take care of herself and her man. Dennis Weaver was another newcomer to television when he was cast as Chester, Dillon's deputy. Weaver went on some years later to star in *McCloud*. Ken Curtis played the crotchety hillbilly deputy. Appearing for a short time was a very young Burt Reynolds as Quint Asper.

The series, which ran as half hour episodes until 1961, was very people-oriented. Most of the stories dealt with the range of people who found their way to Dodge over the years. Through it all, Matt Dillon remained the tower of strength, drawing on his education and church learning to get him through the roughest of times. Viewers at the time seemed especially drawn to this human sort of hero who didn't rely on a gun to solve all of his problems. Matt may have worn a tin badge, but in the TV history books, *Gunsmoke* gets a gold star.

It is interesting to note that in its twenty-year run, *Gunsmoke* was licensed primarily in its first few seasons. Even then it was not licensed by any of the major toy companies such as Remco or Mattel, except for Aladdin, who made it big with four different lunch boxes.

The First Frontier

Gunsmoke Collectibles

			Mint	Ex	Good
COMICS	**Dell/Gold Key**	56-70	40	20	8

Again, Dell did its best with beautiful glossy covers and fresh stories. Look for twenty-seven issues. All issues have a photo of James Arness on the cover.

FIGURE	**Hartland Plastics**	1960s	75	40	22

Another figure from Hartland's "Heroes of the West" series. Came in two sizes, one with a beige horse, and the smaller one with a gray horse.

GAME, BOARD	**Lowell**	195?	100	55	30

Rare board game features a nice cut-out photo of Dillon superimposed over a wagon train being overrun by Indians. In the photo, Dillon bears an amazing resemblance to John Wayne. Game came with a set of small cowboys and Indians so you could act out Custer's last stand all over again.

GAME, TARGET	**Park Plastic**	1958	75	40	22

Plastic dart pistols were included in this kit with several cardboard villains to shoot out. Nice window packaging with a full body shot of Dillon on the left.

			Mint	Ex	Good
HOLSTER SET	**Leslie-Henry**		**500**	**350**	**200**

A double holster set with copper clad grips.

LUNCH BOX	**Aladdin**	**1959**	**150**	**82**	**45**

Another Elmer Lenhardt metal box, this first one of two was trimmed in yellow with a pattern that looked like stitching around the edge. The scene showed Marshal Matt Dillon and deputy firing on a set of bank robbers. They really should be more careful, since two of the robbers are escaping on their horses in the background. It is rumored that Aladdin got hit with a major recall when they realized that first issues of the lunch box had Marshal spelled with an extra "l." If you've got one of these lunch boxes, it should be worth at least double.

LUNCH BOX	**Aladdin**	**1962**	**50**	**27**	**15**

This second shot at *Gunsmoke* came trimmed in red instead of tan.

			Mint	Ex	Good
LUNCH BOX	**Aladdin**	**1972**	**50**	**27**	**15**

This later version is trimmed with the look of a tooled leather band around the edge and has a sketch of Matt riding his horse with his deputy following behind. Nice work, but newer date makes it worth less money.

			Mint	Ex	Good
LUNCH BOX	**Aladdin**	**1973**	**25**	**14**	**8**

Aladdin sure got their money's worth with this license. This last metal box features a sketch of a stagecoach on the back and the same sketch as the 1972 issue on the front.

			Mint	Ex	Good
PISTOL, CAP	**Leslie-Henry**	**1950s**	**135**	**80**	**50**

The Marshal Matt Dillon Gunsmoke Cap Pistol had a ten-inch pop-up cap magazine, a release in front of the triggerguard, scrollwork, and horse-head grips.

			Mint	Ex	Good
PLAY SET	**Marx**	1960	2000	1200	245

The "official" Gunsmoke Dodge City Play Set (#4268, Series 2000). This rare set sells for big money. It contains eighty pieces so you can set up your own Dodge City.

PUZZLE	**Whitman**	1960	30	17	9

One hundred-piece boxed jigsaw puzzle showing Dillon holding back a mob in the jail.

VIEW-MASTER (#B589)	**GAF**		25	21	—

Let's all say it together: three round wheels, 3-D pictures, little paper book. Got it?

THE RIFLEMAN

September 1958 - July 1963

Okay, let's all think about this. Everyone west of the Mississippi knows that Lucas McCain is an expert shot. I mean, how can you miss with a double-barreled Winchester rifle in your hand? Yet every week, some fool cowboy comes to town and challenges him to a gunfight. Lucas always says, "No, I can't. It's against my principles." Then the guy pushes it by kidnapping his son or robbing the local bank. Then, like it's some great surprise, McCain blows the guy away without even working up a sweat. Now, if I were a bank robber, the last thing I would do is ride into North Fork and announce my intentions to a crack shot with a rifle. Maybe it's a guy thing.

Seriously, *The Rifleman* was more than just a shoot-'em-up cowboy show. The charm of *The Rifleman* lay in the relationship between Lucas (Chuck Connors) and his son Mark (teen singing star Johnny Crawford). It was the bond between them that kept viewers tuning in week after week. They lived in a modest cabin, they worked hard seven days a week, and money was a luxury rarely seen. But they didn't complain (well, Mark did occasionally) and they thanked God each night, knowing in their hearts that things could be worse. Most of *The Rifleman*'s episodes can be linked to one of the Ten Commandments. Thou Shalt Not Kill: "The Sheridan Story." Thou Shalt Not Steal: "The Safe Guard." Thou Shalt Not Covet Thy Neighbor's Wife: "The Obituary." *The Rifleman* was often criticized for being too moralistic and overly preachy, but underneath the storylines were lessons children could learn even in the nineties.

Softening the look of the show were two ladies who were added as love interests for Lucas. (No, not at the same time.) Joan Taylor played Miss Milly Scott, the good-hearted homey type who ran the general store. She was followed by Patricia Blair as Lou Mallory. Lou was a little wilder, making her introduction as a con woman, but ending up as the owner of the local hotel that Lucas and Mark frequented. While Lou was lots of fun, Miss Milly added a nice feminine touch that the show was lacking. The episodes that feature her and her relationship to the McCains are particularly sweet. When it comes to tearjerkers, check out "The Vision," which has Mark dreaming of his dead mother as he battles typhoid fever. Then there's "Panic," where the McCains open their home to a young couple suspected of carrying yellow fever. This is a particularly strong episode that exposes the ugly side of humanity when we are driven by fear of the unknown.

With every little boy in America wanting to be Lucas McCain, and every little girl wanting to marry Mark McCain, toy manufacturers had no trouble selling *Rifleman* merchandise. One of the best finds is a *Rifleman* playsuit that consisted of a flannel shirt, felt chaps, and assorted cowboy gear. Considered a very hot item in 1959, kids today wouldn't be caught dead running around the neighborhood in a cowboy outfit, but I bet Dad still tries on his old holster every chance he gets.

Rifleman Collectibles

			Mint	Ex	Good
COMICS	Dell/Gold Key	59-64	60	30	10

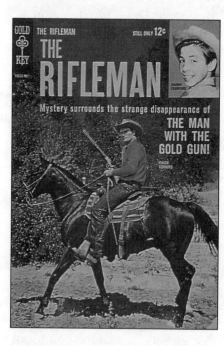

Dell comics was number one for TV tie-in comics, so *Rifleman* was a natural. Look for quality photo covers and original stories. It's interesting to note that twenty issues were released after the series' cancellation.

			Mint	Ex	Good
FIGURE	Hartland	1960	100	55	30

Plastic figure on a horse that was made as part of Hartland's cowboy series, which included other men of the West like Wyatt Earp and Cochise.

			Mint	Ex	Good
GAME, BOARD	Milton Bradley	1959	75	40	25

Typical board game. The box lid contains nice graphics of Lucas pushing Mark out of the way as he prepares to blow away a bad guy. Not exactly "Go to the Head of the Class."

			Mint	Ex	Good
GUN	**Hubley**	**1959**	**125**	**70**	**40**

Plastic replica of Lucas's Winchester. The gun was made to fire caps.

LUNCH BOX	**Aladdin**	**1961**	**200**	**110**	**60**

Another metal graduate from the Elmer Lenhardt school of box painting. There is a nice action scene on the front showing Lucas attempting to apprehend several bank robbers on their way out of the bank. Mark is shown cowering behind a rain barrel while a woman in the bank cries in horror. Notice that the first bandit is holding his wrist, his gun on the ground in front of him, giving the impression that Lucas has just shot the gun out of his hand. I can almost hear the Winchester firing now!

PAINT SET	**Standard Toykraft**	**1960**	**125**	**70**	**40**

A chance to dabble in the arts between shootings, this "TV Stage" paint-by-number set (10" x 15" box) came with seven oil paints and several cutouts to paint. The cutouts could be assembled to create your own miniature North Fork. This set also came in a Deluxe version with more paints and more cutouts in a bigger box. Expect to pay upwards of $50 more for this version.

PLAY SET	**Marx**	**1959**	**700**	**385**	**210**

The price tag on this one represents the popularity of Marx play sets. Marx perfected the art of doll houses for boys. This kit comes with two tin houses, several figures, lots of fences, horses, a covered wagon, a water pump, and lots of little accessories for riding your own range. The set must have been based on a McCain dream ranch since the Marx play set has more stuff than Lucas ever owned.

PLAYSUIT	**Pla-Master**	**1959**	**300**	**165**	**90**

Now here's something you don't see anymore, an official licensed cowboy outfit. (Dallas Cowboy maybe, but certainly not this kind.) This set came with a fringed shirt made of flannel, a set of felt chaps, and a felt cowboy hat. Pieces of the outfit bore the *Rifleman* logo and a photo of Lucas McCain. I'll bet this was a big seller on Halloween.

ZORRO

October 1957 - September 1959

(Re-released in the sixties on *Walt Disney Presents*)

In 1958, kids all over America could be found scribbling Zs all over the sidewalk, the school yard, and the walls of their bedroom. Thus graffiti was born. Responsible for all this frenzy was an unknown thirty-three-year-old actor named Guy Williams and a simple production company known as Disney. With the success of *Davy Crockett*, the studio decided to try a series based on the adventures of Zorro, a story that had filled the pages of comic books for many years. Zorro was a masked avenger with a wit as sharp as his saber. The story goes that Williams got the part of Zorro because he was an expert fencer and Walt Disney insisted on staging the fight scenes with unprotected fencing foils. When not running around scratching Zs into everything, Zorro assumed his real identity as Don Diego de la Vega (by the time you call him he's late for dinner). Diego was the son of a rich nobleman in Spanish California in 1920. He played the part of a lazy, self-centered rich boy to keep people from discovering his secret. The only one to know the truth was his mute manservant Bernardo. The servant, pretending to be deaf, was Zorro's main pipeline to all the gossip in the town. Now don't think Zorro was liked by everyone. His arch enemy, not counting bank robbers and assassins, was the commandant of the Fortress de los Angeles (get the joke?), Capt. Monastario, played by Britt Lomond. Henry Calvin played assistant bad guy Sgt. Garcia. A comical character, Garcia was short, fat, blundering, and the spitting image of Oliver Hardy.

When Disney devised the series, they were not convinced of its success so they took a few shortcuts, like filming the show in black and white, to save money. Much to their surprise, *Zorro* was a huge hit for ABC. In 1958, Disney cut a deal with NBC to move all of their programming onto the new, more modern network. NBC had just created its new logo, the infamous NBC peacock, with an announcement that all of the shows on NBC would be broadcast in living color. Since *Zorro* was filmed in black and white, Disney was forced to give up the series rather than lose the exposure for their new show, *Walt Disney Presents* (later to be *The World of Color*). The move they made to save money cost them their most popular show.

In the aftermath of *Zorro*, Guy Williams auditioned to play Adam Cartwright on *Bonanza*. Although he didn't get the part, he was asked to join the series for several episodes when actor Pernell Roberts began threatening to quit. Soon after, Williams was cast as John Robinson in *Lost in Space*. Although he is probably better known for his *Lost in Space* role today, at the time, Williams never achieved the kind of fame and standing he had while playing Zorro. When *Lost in Space* ended its run, the actor moved to Argentina, where he was welcomed as a national hero, just as if he were really Zorro. For years he made appearances in costume. In the end, Guy Williams became a recluse, rarely leaving his home in Argentina. He died of a heart attack in 1989.

When collecting *Zorro*, there are several different eras of toys. Most toys were made in the late fifties to fit the first release of the show. Then in the sixties, a second round of toys were made to tie in to Disney's re-release of the series on a kind of mini-series basis. In the eighties, a whole new batch of toys were made to promote a new *Zorro* comedy movie and a re-creation of the series on television with Duncan Regher in the lead.

All the collectibles are fun, but none of the modern toys have the value of an original *Zorro* piece from the fifties.

Zorro Collectibles

			Mint	Ex	Good
ACTION SET	**Marx**	**1958**	**400**	**220**	**120**

Wonderful play set with everything you need to be Zorro—plastic hat, mask, whip, and knife. And how many kids can own their own fencing foil and flintlock pistol? The swords were chalk tipped so you could make the sign of the Z on the side of your house. A true historical treasure. An exclusive to Grant's department store.

			Mint	Ex	Good
BEAN BAG GAME	**Gardner Toys**	**1960**	**100**	**55**	**30**

This one is rare mainly because it came from a small toy company. The game is a pretty silly thing with a poor sketch of Zorro inside the box surrounded by cups and targets. You could throw Zorro bean bags at the target or fire suction cup darts. But the real question is: Why would you want to shoot AT Zorro?

			Mint	Ex	Good
BOOK	**Golden Book**	**1958**	**10**	**6**	**3**

A Little Golden Book. *Walt Disney's Zorro* states that "The exciting tale of Zorro the fox takes place in Spanish California of the early 1800s."

			Mint	Ex	Good
COMICS	**Dell**	**59-61**	**100**	**55**	**30**

Once again, beautiful color covers and good stories. The issue with Annette Funicello on the cover is particularly sought after.

COMICS	**Gold Key**	**66-68**	**30**	**15**	**5**

Nine issues, all reprints of the Dell versions, but not as nice.

COSTUME	**Ben Cooper**	**1958**	**200**	**110**	**60**

The costume was a sure winner for little boys of the era even though the mask gives Zorro a rather frightening toothy grin.

GAME, BOARD	**Whitman**	**1965**	**30**	**17**	**9**

Here's a cheap idea for a box: take a shot of a bunch of kids playing the game, add a blown up version of the logo, and ta-daaa, box art! This educational game challenges you to collect the cards that spell Zorro. (Tough one, huh?) The board's path is in the shape of, you guessed it, a "Z."

			Mint	Ex	Good
GAME, BOARD	**Parker Bros.**	**1966**	**50**	**27**	**15**

Box art shows Zorro, sword held high, horse rearing, with the Spanish city in the far background. The object of this game is to reach the end. Parker Bros. doesn't believe in complicating matters.

GAME, TARGET	**Knickerbocker**	**1950s**	**50**	**30**	**20**

Came with a dart gun.

GUM CARDS	**Topps**	**1958**	**250**	**140**	**75**

The Zorro cards possess a hand-painted look, with photos from the series, and captions. It's interesting that these old cards are color, as early sixties TV cards are generally black and white.

LUNCH BOX	**Aladdin**	**1958**	**100**	**55**	**30**

This early version of the lunch box is not embossed and has a beautiful stormy blue and orange sky in the background with Zorro in his famous pose. The thermos has a black cap and shows Don Diego mid-swordfight.

LUNCH BOX	**Aladdin**	**1966**	**100**	**55**	**30**

This later edition of the box is basically the same pose, but the sky is an unflattering red and Zorro is facing more forward. The thermos has a red lid. Even though this box is embossed, it's not nearly as nice as the earlier version.

		Mint	Ex	Good
MODEL Aurora	1965	300	165	90

This one is gorgeous! The box is a wonderful painting of Zorro in his usual pose. The color is intense and worth the price of admission. The kit itself is a very detailed action pose and it's extremely easy to paint. Everything is black!

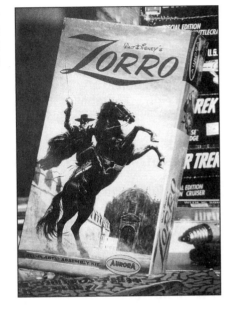

		Mint	Ex	Good
PAINT SET Hassenfeld	1960	75	40	22

A beautiful painting of Zorro on his horse graces the lid of the paint set, which came with four canvases to paint and a set of oils.

	Mint	Ex	Good
PEZ CANDY DISPENSER Pez-Haas, Inc.	50	25	—

This Zorro likeness has no feet, flesh-colored face, and black mask and hat.

	Mint	Ex	Good
PEZ CANDY DISPENSER Pez-Haas, Inc.	75	75	—

Zorro with no feet, black mask and hat, and Zorro logo on stem.

		Mint	Ex	Good
PLAY SET Marx	1958	1200	660	360

Nice boxed play set depicting a Spanish style town with tin buildings, trees, fences, and figures, including Zorro on his horse. Number 3753.

			Mint	Ex	Good
PUNCH-OUT BOOK	Pocket Books	1958	50	27	15

Basically paper dolls for boys. Tall 7" x 13" size has a nice action sketch of Zorro leaping from a balcony onto his horse.

			Mint	Ex	Good
PUZZLE, JIGSAW	Jaymar	1958	40	22	12

Boxed puzzle features a sketch of Zorro on the left with a replica of the puzzle photo on the right. The photos have that nice late fifties hand-colored look. Four styles were released: Flashing Steel, Sgt. Garcia and Diego, The Avenger, and The Duel.

			Mint	Ex	Good
SECRET SIGHT SCARF MASK	Westminster	1960	75	50	25

A black fabric mask with black/silver hard plastic eyepieces.

			Mint	Ex	Good
TARGET SET	T Cohn	1960	200	110	60

This metal target is well-crafted with a painting of Zorro fighting a swarm of Mexican desperados. A twenty-one-inch rifle came with the set, along with a pair of suction cup darts.

			Mint	Ex	Good
VIEW-MASTER (#B469)	GAF	1958	40	34	—

The usual, but the package is done in the old style with a small picture framed on the left and a description on the right.

Prices are for mint condition. Excellent: 55% of mint; good: 30%.

Stymie Card Game. Milton Bradley, 1964. $30.

Munsters Paper Dolls. Whitman, 1966. $60.

Munsters Hand Puppets. Unknown, 1964. $100.

Addams Family Board Game. Ideal, 1964. $50.

Munsters Koach. AMT, 1964. $250.

Munsters Comics. Gold Key, 1965-68. NM $50.

Munsters Dolls. Remco, 1964. $100.

Prices are for mint condition. Excellent: 55% of mint; good: 30%.

Family Affair Paper Dolls. Whitman, 1970. $30.

Get Smart Comics. Dell, 1966-67. $40.

Get Smart Paperback. Tempo Books, 1965. VG $7.

Family Affair Board Game. Whitman, 1971. $30.

Get Smart Card Game. Ideal, 1966. $40.

The Monkees Game. Transogram, 1967. $75.

Right: *The Monkees Go Mod*. Popular Library, 1967. VG $5.

Get Smart Lunch Box. King Seeley, 1966. $100.

Beverly Hillbillies Card Game. Milton Bradley, 1963. $50.

Prices are for mint condition. Excellent: 55% of mint; good: 30%.

Star Trek Game. Ideal, 1967. $100.

Lost in Space Game. Milton Bradley, 1965. $75.

Lost in Space Roto-Jet Gun. Mattel, 1966. $2500.

Star Trek Book. Bantam Books, 1967. VG $10.

Lost in Space Diorama Model. Aurora, 1966. $1200.

Voyage to the Bottom of the Sea Comics. Dell/ Gold Key, 1961-70. $20.

Outer Limits Comics. Dell, 1964-69. $15.

Voyage to the Bottom of the Sea Hardcover Book. Whitman, 1965. VG $5.

Dark Shadows Paperback Novels. Dell. $15.

Left: Dark Shadows Comics. Gold Key, 1969-76. $40.

Prices are for mint condition. Excellent: 55% of mint; good: 30%.

Land of the Giants Board Game. Ideal, 1968. $150.

Spindrift Model. Aurora, 1968. $1000.

Land of the Giants Comics. Gold Key, 1968. $20.

Spindrift Toothpick Kit. Remco, 1968. $125.

Land of the Giants Snake Model Kit. Aurora, 1968. $1000.

Land of the Giants Lunch Box. Aladdin, 1969. $250.

Land of the Giants Colorforms. Colorforms, 1968. $125.

Land of the Giants Target Rifle. Remco, 1968. $400.

Prices are for mint condition. Excellent: 55% of mint; good: 30%.

Gunsmoke Board Game. Lowell, 1950s. $100.

Lorne Greene Record Album. RCA Victor, 1964. NM $20.

Bonanza Comics. Dell/ Gold Key, 1960-70. $30.

The Rifleman Game. Milton Bradley, 1959. $75.

Bonanza Model. Revell, 1966. $175.

Rifleman "Flip Special" Gun. Hubley, 1959. $125.

Rifleman Comics. Dell/ Gold Key, 1959-64. $60.

Zorro Game. Parker Bros., 1966. $50.

Zorro Book. Little Golden Book, 1958. $10.

Zorro Play Set. Marx, 1958. $1200.

Prices are for mint condition. Excellent: 55% of mint; good: 30%.

Dr. Kildare Comics.
Dell, 1962-65. $30.

Green Hornet Comics.
Gold Key, 1967. $80.

A Biography of Vince Edwards. Belmont, 1962. VG $6.

Ben Casey: A Rage for Justice. 1962. VG $7.

Green Hornet Charm Bracelet. Greenway, 1966. $180.

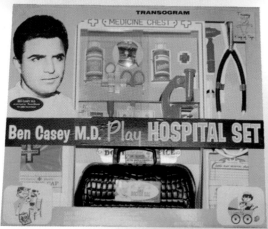

Ben Casey Play Hospital Set. Transogram, 1962. $50.

Green Hornet PEZ
Dispenser. Pez-Haas, Inc.
$200.

Green Hornet Color-
forms. Colorforms,
1966. $80.

Green Hornet Lunch Box. King Seeley, 1967. $250.

Green Hornet Quick Switch Game. Milton
Bradley, 1966. $80.

Prices are for mint condition. Excellent: 55% of mint; good: 30%.

Green Hornet
Car. Corgi, 1966.
$250.

Green Hornet Playing
Cards. Ed-U-Cards,
1966. $50.

Green Hornet Movie
Viewer. Chemtoy, 1966.
$45.

Man from U.N.C.L.E.
Figure Models. Aurora,
1966. $500 each.

Green Hornet Wrist
Radios. Remco, 1966.
$200.

Below: Illya Kuryakin
Gun Set. Ideal, 1965.
$200.

Man from U.N.C.L.E. Spy Magic Tricks. Gilbert,
1965. $475.

Napoleon Solo Gun Set. Ideal, 1965. $600.

Left: Man from
U.N.C.L.E. Foto
Fantastiks. Eberhard
Faber, 1965. $75.

Right: Batman Lunch
Box. Aladdin, 1966.
$150.

Prices are for mint condition. Excellent: 55% of mint; good: 30%.

Rat Patrol Play Set. Remco, 1967. $200.

Rat Patrol Costume. Ben Cooper, 1967. $100.

Rat Patrol Diorama Model Kit. Aurora, 1967. $125.

Rat Patrol Lunch Box and Thermos. Aladdin, 1967. $65.

Combat Play Set. Superior Toys, 1963. $250.

Rat Patrol Coloring Book. Saalfield, 1966. $40.

Heroes, Spies and Medical Men:

Drama and Adventure on Television

In 1960 a horrible thing happened. Television ran out of good ideas. The Western, which had been so popular in the fifties, was beginning its downhill spiral. The top ten were taken up by an odd mix of shows like *Candid Camera*, *The Price is Right* and *The Jack Benny Show*. Networks came up with this bundle of hits: *Klondike*, *Dante*, *Peck's Bad Girl*, *Mr. Garlund* and *Dan Raven*. I'll give you a gold star if you can name the leads in any of those shows. Anthology series like *Alcoa Presents* and *The Bell Telephone Hour* took the label of "drama," presenting us with stage productions that were merely simulations of real life.

"Real life" was becoming much more exciting than a TV show. Track star Wilma Rudolph won three gold medals at the Olympics in Rome, NASA launched the first weather satellite, and the Russians shot down alleged spy Gary Powers. Then Americans were treated to their first televised presidential debate, between John F. Kennedy and Richard Nixon. (They say TV got Kennedy elected.) It was time for television to change. Viewers were tired of soap operas; they wanted to see real life heroes. This provided the networks with the gimmick they had been looking for. They gave us doctors fighting for their patients in *Dr. Kildare*, *Ben Casey* and *The Nurses*. They gave us lawyers fighting for the rights of their clients in *The Defenders* and *Perry Mason*. They gave us cops fighting for the rights of people on the streets in *Hawaii Five-O* and *Burke's Law*. They gave us people to believe in.

As we moved into the mid-sixties, the title of dramatic series became a little muddy. Our heroes were larger than life and not quite so average anymore. Parodies like *Batman*, *The Man from U.N.C.L.E.* and *Wild Wild West* reigned supreme. All of these shows had a comic bent, but they didn't have any of the earmarks of situation comedies of the era. These shows were usually an hour long (put together the two halves of a Batman episode to qualify), their sets were varied, and the action was wild.

The gamut was run throughout the sixties, and unfortunately there were no VCRs. On Friday nights in 1966 you could watch either *The Green Hornet*, *Wild Wild West* or *Tarzan*, followed by *The Time Tunnel* or *The Man from U.N.C.L.E.* and *T.H.E. CAT*. How could a person choose! Although 1966 was probably the best year television ever had, it was not without its flops. Who can name the two famous actors who starred in *Hawk* and *Shane*, two of the season's shortest living series (less than three months for each)? (Check the bottom of the page for the answer.)

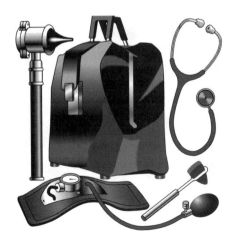

(Hawk was played by Burt Reynolds and Shane by David Carradine)

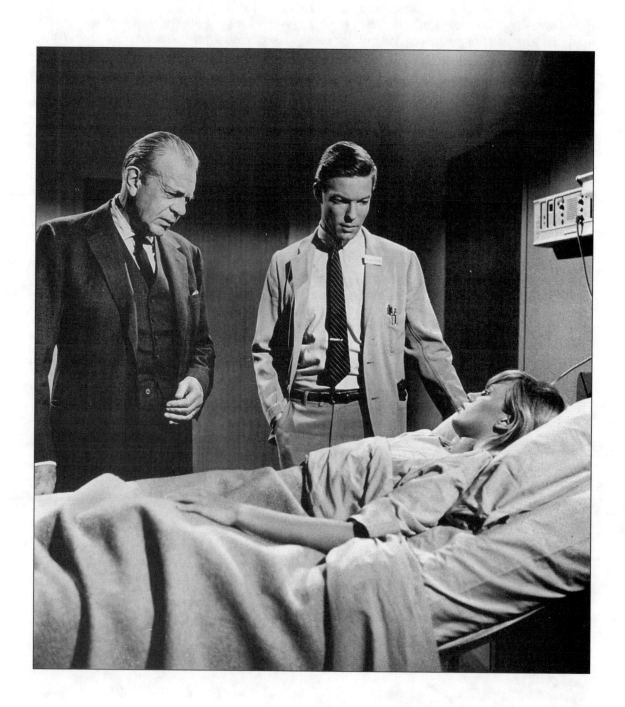

DR. KILDARE

September 1961 - August 1966

BEN CASEY

October 1961 - March 1966

In 1961 a very odd thing happened. Two production companies each developed a doctor series for television. In an era when doctors were mostly seen on the daytime soaps, *Dr. Kildare* and *Ben Casey* gave nighttime viewers a chance to see what they were missing. *Dr. Kildare* (KIL - DARE, is that supposed to be some kind of doctor pun?) was actually a TV version of a series of movies made in the forties. On TV, Kildare was a young intern in the big city hospital Blair General. Playing the part was the baby-faced newcomer Richard Chamberlain. Giving him advice and counsel was his mentor and friend, Dr. Gillespie, played by veteran movie actor Raymond Massey. The stories dealt with the gritty realities of life and death, the bureaucracy against the doctor sworn to save lives. Chamberlain's honest innocence appealed to more than just teenyboppers. Rumor has it the Polish Communist Party rescheduled their meeting night so it wouldn't conflict with the series. Chamberlain's face graced the cover of every movie magazine in town and he even launched a singing career with the show's theme, "Three Stars Will Shine Tonight." As the show moved forward, Kildare became a resident and the plots moved away from the lives of the doctors and onto the lives of the patients. In its last season, the show was aired twice a week, on Monday and Tuesday, for a half hour each night. This was obviously some strange attempt to save the series. (On a side note, look for episodes written by future *Star Trek* creator Gene Roddenberry.)

Given the formula for success, one would think *Ben Casey* was a carbon copy of *Kildare*, but that isn't so. Yes, it's still a doctor show set in a big city hospital, County General to be exact. And yes, Casey did have his own mentor, Dr. Zorba, played by wild-eyed Sam Jaffee, but that is where the likenesses end. Vince Edwards, who starred as Casey, was a Brooklyn boy; Chamberlain was born in Beverly Hills. Casey faced his problems with more venom and vim. The style of the series was more intense, with a lot of tight close-ups and soap opera style reaction shots. Casey was a surgeon intent on saving lives no matter who he had to step on to do it. Kildare might have been a by-the-book doctor, but Casey was a throw-away-the-book man. He was daring and aggressive. With his open shirt and hairy chest, Edwards had his own share of teeny-

bopper fans. By 1965, Dr. Zorba departed and was replaced by Dr. Daniel Freeland, played by Franchot Tone. Cliffhangers were introduced and the soap opera quality ruled supreme. At one point in the story line, Casey even had a love affair with a woman who had just awakened from a thirteen-year coma. (Strange trivia for *Ben Casey*: Bing Crosby discovered Edwards and produced the series.)

"Man, woman, birth, death, infinity," so sayeth Dr. Zorba. In the circle of life and death, *Kildare* and *Casey* were intertwined like a pair of Siamese twins. They were born together in 1961 and oddly died within six months of each other in 1966.

Dr. Kildare Collectibles

			Mint	Ex	Good
COMICS	Dell	62-65	30	15	6

Only nine issues—this time all nice photo covers and good stories with Richard Chamberlain's photo on the cover.

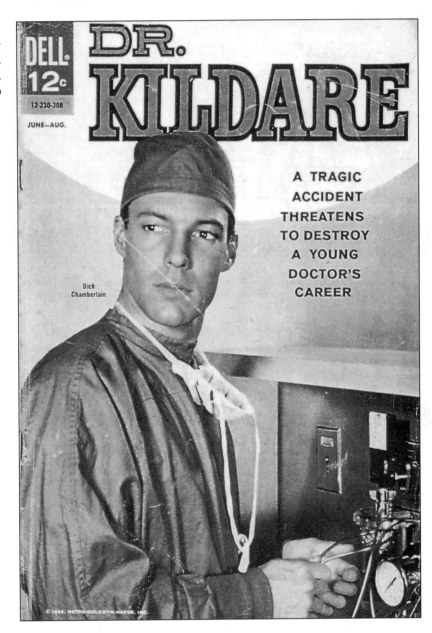

GAME	Ideal	1963	75	40	22

The Dr. Kildare Perilous Night Game was part of a series of envelope games made by Ideal. Since the game was contained in an oversized envelope it was easily destroyed, thus it commands a higher price than most games of the era. Look for a nice photo of Richard Chamberlain on the front.

			Mint	Ex	Good
GAME, BOARD	**Ideal**	**1962**	**30**	**17**	**9**

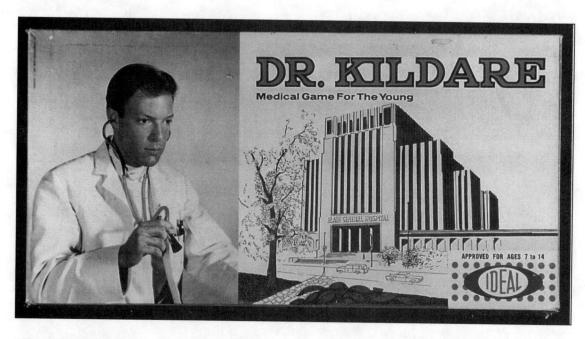

Here's a winner: The Doctor Kildare Game for the Young. Don't tell me, it must take place on the children's ward. To win, follow the board and diagnose your patients before they die.

PHOTO SCRAPBOOK		**1962**	**45**	**25**	**10**
PUNCH-OUT BOOK	**Golden**	**1962**	**30**	**17**	**9**

The Junior Doctor Kit was kind of a paper hospital you could punch out and use.

PUNCH-OUT BOOK	**Collins**	**1965**	**40**	**22**	**12**

Dr. Kildare and Nurse Susan are the topics of this paper doll book printed in England.

PUZZLE, JIGSAW	**Milton Bradley**	**1962**	**30**	**17**	**9**

These boxed 100-piece puzzles were sketches based on the TV series.

STETHOSCOPE	**Amson**	**1962**	**50**	**27**	**15**

The Dr. Kildare Thumpy-The HeartBeat Stethoscope was sure to make you popular on the block. After all, what better way to convince the neighbor girl to play doctor? The toy came shrink-wrapped to a card with the earpieces inserted in the ears of a photo of Kildare.

Ben Casey Collectibles

			Mint	Ex	Good
BOOK		1962	—	7	—

Ben Casey: A Rage for Justice. The book's cover states, "A new novel by Norman Daniels based on the big ABC-TV show. Free inside this book 7 x 10 pin-up of Vince Edwards."

BOOK, PAPERBACK	**Belmont**	1962	—	6	—

A Biography of Vince Edwards, Television's Ben Casey by George Carpozi, Jr. This was advertised as "the irreverent, unbiased and unauthorized book about TV's most famous doctor and his colleagues."

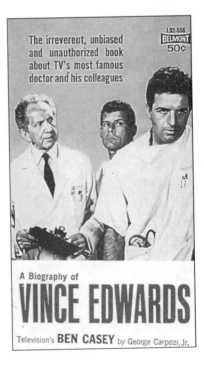

			Mint	Ex	Good
COLORING BOOK	Saalfield		25	15	10
COMICS	Dell	1962-65	20	10	5

There were ten regular issues of the comics. One special all-photo issue, called "The Ben Casey Film Story," was released in November 1962.

GAME	Transogram	1961	40	22	12

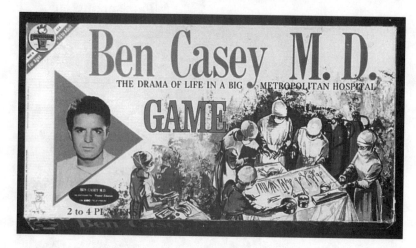

The Ben Casey game was subtitled "The Drama of Life in a Big Metropolitan Hospital." There is a sketch of the surgical team in action with a photo of Edwards on the left.

HOSPITAL CART	Transogram	1962	300	165	90

This beats all. This large box contained a wheeled cart with its very own plasma stand and bottle, forceps, blood pressure gauge, thermometer and more. Now you can take your friend's temperature and draw blood all in the comfort of your own home.

PLAY SET	Transogram	1962	50	27	15

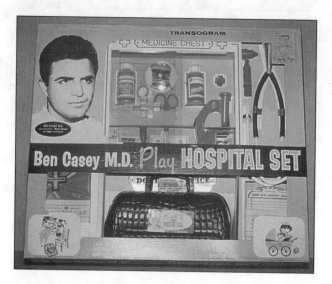

This play hospital set came with a doctor's bag full of instruments and charts and a doctor's cap. Obviously from an era when doctors still made house calls.

		Mint	Ex	Good
PLAYSUIT	Unknown	**75**	**40**	**22**

This boxed set contained a child's set of scrubs with the name "Ben Casey" embroidered over the pocket. It came with a stethoscope so you could compete with your friend Dr. Kildare.

SWEATER GUARD	Gerald Sears Co. 1962	—	—	**10**

Here's an important accessory for every young female teen in the sixties! Dangling from the chain were charms of the biological symbols for man, woman, birth, death, and infinity.

GREEN HORNET

September 1966 - July 1967

When that bee starts to buzz, he's not making honey, he's making MONEY. As in GREEN. As in *The Green Hornet*, another millionaire playboy out fighting crime. This time it's Britt Reid, grand-nephew of the Lone Ranger, John Reid. (I guess fighting bad guys runs in the family.) Reid was portrayed with boyish charm by Van Williams, who had previously starred in *Bourbon Street Beat*. Like other superheroes of the day, Reid was living a double life. By day he was the publisher of the *Daily Sentinel*, by night he transformed (donning a long coat and a silly half mask) into the bane of all evildoers— the Green Hornet. In an interesting character twist, the Green Hornet was considered a villain by many and was apparently wanted by the police. It was Reid's good friend, District Attorney Scanlon, played by Walter Brooke, who covered the truth, allowing him to evade capture by the police. Assisting GH (his friends call him GH) was his faithful servant and chauffeur, Kato. Martial arts legend Bruce Lee made his TV debut as Reid's side "kick" (all puns intended). Thanks to his appearance at a Kung Fu tournament, Lee was originally hired by 20th Century Fox to play Charlie Chan's number one son in a new series they were producing. He was screen-tested and sent to acting school, then suddenly the Charlie Chan role was out and Kato was in. Sharing the spotlight with Williams and Lee was Black Beauty (no, not the horse), a customized 1966 Chrysler Imperial that included such features as an ice spreader to deter tailgaters, a sweeper to erase tire tracks and special green headlights for driving in the dark, which was the only time the Green Hornet came out to play. Like the famous Batmobile, Black Beauty was hidden underneath Reid's home, but its appearance was much more fanciful. When Kato was ready to roll, he activated a secret switch that made Reid's normal car trade places with Black Beauty by means of a rotating floor. Once out and about, the Green Hornet could be seen using his Hornet gun, which fired a green knockout gas. For meaner enemies, he might use the Hornet sting, which fired a laser beam that could blow a lock off a door. As for Kato, all he needed were those famous flying feet. Watching Bruce Lee fight is one of best reasons to watch the series.

Although *The Green Hornet* was often compared to its big cousin *Batman*, the similarities were few. While *Batman* was funky and colorful, *Green Hornet* was dark and cynical. Both shows were produced by William Dozier, but it is plain to see he had a different task in mind for each. No pasty-faced comic book villains in *The Green Hornet*. Most of the stories involved mobsters, bootleggers, and gangs. The plots were closer to that of *Dick Tracy* or *The Untouchables*, both of which began on the radio alongside *The Green Hornet*. For best in show, check out "The Praying Mantis," with its guest star Mako and "Alias The Scarf" with the wonderfully creepy John Carradine.

Green Hornet Collectibles

			Mint	Ex	Good
BOOK	**Whitman**		45	30	13

The Green Hornet Strikes!

			Mint	Ex	Good
BUBBLE GUM CARDS	**Donruss**	1966	150	82	45

The Green Hornet set is made up of forty-four color photo cards. The backs formed a puzzle when put together. The wrapper was the logo with the hornet (the insect, not the guy) and those psychedelic lines again. The box uses a nice sketch of Kato, the Hornet, and Black Beauty. Expect to pay $50 for a wrapper, $100 for a box.

			Mint	Ex	Good
BUBBLE GUM RING	**Frito Lay**		90	45	20

A rubber ring in a cello pak.

			Mint	Ex	Good
CAR	**Corgi**	1966	250	140	75

Another hit from Corgi: a metal replica of the Black Beauty. You'll find the Green Hornet in the back seat and Kato at the wheel. The car was designed to launch missiles and radar scanning discs. The box is uneventful but the car is truly cool.

		Mint	Ex	Good
CARDS, PLAYING Ed-U-Cards	1966	50	27	15

This set of "educational" playing cards is actually a full deck with great photos from the series on the front of each. The oddest cards are the face cards, as they have cut-out photo heads of the cast superimposed over the usual sketched bodies. Kato is the jack, Reid's secretary Casey is the queen, and of course, the Hornet is the king.

CHARM BRACELET Greenway	1966	180	90	45

A gold finish chain with five charms: Hornet, Van, Kato, Pistol, and Black Beauty. Came on a 3" x 7" illustrated card.

			Mint	Ex	Good
COLORFORMS	**Colorforms**	**1966**	**80**	**45**	**25**

You know the bit, vinyl stick-on people with a static background. The box art shows the Hornet being particularly aggressive in the use of his Hornet Gun.

COLORING BOOK	**Whitman**	**1966**	**30**	**17**	**9**

This book is orange with green letters and three nice color photos from the series. The coloring book is a thick one with a story about the kidnapping of a young prince.

			Mint	Ex	Good
COMICS	**Gold Key**	**1967**	**80**	**40**	**15**

There were only three Green Hornet comics is-sued that were based on the television series. There are, however, dozens of comics based on the original character, some of which sell for upwards of $300.

			Mint	Ex	Good
COSTUME	**Ben Cooper**	**1966**	**200**	**110**	**60**

Basic one-piece jumpsuit with a plastic mask of a face wearing a plastic mask (cosmic, huh?). Only one question: Where's Kato? I mean, who wants to be a chauffeur for Hal-loween?

			Mint	Ex	Good
DRAWING SET	**Lakeside**	**1966**	**200**	**110**	**60**

An electric light table with a logo on top became a Green Hornet Drawing Set for Lake-side. The original set came with illustrations to trace and finding these is the tough part. The box is almost two feet long and bears a nice sketch of our heroes and their car.

			Mint	Ex	Good
FIGURE	**Lakeside**	**1966**	**40**	**22**	**12**

This bendable (a la Gumby) figure came shrink-wrapped on a card. The figure is dressed properly, although a bit flat for my taste, and came with the proclamation "Sits, stands, twists and bends into thousands of action positions" on the card. Person-ally, I could only make it sit, bend, and twist into 346 positions, but who's counting.

			Mint	Ex	Good
FLASHER PIN	**GPI**	**1967**	**30**	**17**	**9**

Plastic eight-inch pin was designed as a flasher that changed from the Hornet's face to a mad hornet, each surrounded by the psychedelic wave pattern from the show's opening.

			Mint	Ex	Good
FLASHER RINGS	Chemtoy	1960s	120	60	30

The rings had silver bands and came in eight designs: Hornet Sting, Kato and GH in action, GH running with hostage, Hornet logo, Black Beauty/TV logo, Kato running down a thief, GH and Miss Case. Price is for each.

			Mint	Ex	Good
GAME, BOARD	Milton Bradley	1966	80	45	25

The Green Hornet Quick Switch Game was designed with four wheels, one on each corner of the board, facing into a very sixties centerpiece with the show's title repeated in two directions. The unusual nature of the board makes this one a little pricier than most games of the era.

			Mint	Ex	Good
GREEN HORNET COSTUME FOR CAPTAIN ACTION DOLL	Ideal	1966	5000	1400	700

The closest thing you'll come to finding a Green Hornet action figure is to dress Ideal's Captain Action doll in the Green Hornet costume, which was sold separately. The costume is a rare find, and commands up to $5000 mint in the box.

			Mint	Ex	Good
LUNCH BOX	**King Seeley**	**1967**	**250**	**140**	**75**

It's GREEEEEN! Like you would expect anything different. Actually, the Green Hornet lunch box is one of the best. Its artwork is clean and colorful. There is a nice action shot of Kato and the Hornet doing in a couple of bad guys in suits on the front. The back is a shot of the Black Beauty that is so well done you can see the reflection of the city lights in the side of the car. It has the look of 3-D even though it is not an embossed lunch box. The two sides show Kato and the Hornet in their costumes, while the bottom (yes, the bottom) of the box shows them out of their disguises enjoying a quiet evening at home.

			Mint	Ex	Good
MAGIC SLATES	**Whitman**	**1966**	**80**	**45**	**25**

Another nothing toy in a cool box. Eight glossy slates came in the box with a set of wipe-off crayons and a cloth. The box has a nice close-up sketch of the Hornet with two children having hours of fun in the background.

			Mint	Ex	Good
MODEL, CAR	**Aurora**	**1966**	**400**	**220**	**120**

The artwork on the box is not up to Aurora's usual standard, but the model is a nice detailed version of the Black Beauty and it sells for a few bucks even with its bland packaging.

			Mint	Ex	Good
MOVIE VIEWER	**Chemtoy**	**1966**	**45**	**25**	**15**

Part of a line of small viewers made by Chemtoy. Each came with two very tiny rolls of film with a cartoon based on the series. The kind of thing you found at the Woolworth's counter for fifty cents.

			Mint	Ex	Good
PAINT SET	**Hasbro**	**1966**	**200**	**110**	**60**

Hasbro made two different paint sets for the budding crime fighting artist to work on in his spare time. One was a paint-by-number and the other, get ready, the Hornet on Velvet. They just don't make them like that any more.

			Mint	Ex	Good

PEZ CANDY DISPENSER Pez-Haas, Inc.   200   150   —

This PEZ had no feet and featured the Green Hornet wearing a green mask and his standard hat.

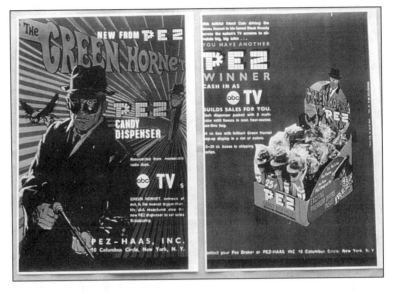

PRINT PUTTY	**Colorforms**	1966	50	27	15

Now here's a rip-off if I ever heard of one. This is a piece of silly putty in a really puffed up package. The card shows the Hornet gun shooting at a plastic canister of the putty. There is a picture of Kato and the Hornet underneath and the words "Bounce it, stretch it, now print with it!" Remember how silly putty would lift and transfer fingerprints and newspaper print? I wonder how the guys in the crime lab get along without it.

PUZZLES, TRAY	**Whitman**	1966	75	40	22

Boxed set of four puzzles showed the Green Hornet in and out of trouble. Tough to find with all the pieces.

			Mint	Ex	Good
STICKERS	**Topps**	**1966**	**100**	**55**	**30**

Packaged like bubble gum cards, this set of forty-four stickers had a bit more flash than their counterpart. The photos were set into frames of varied shapes, like ovals, zigzags, or diamonds. Most featured the show's title on the frame, but one particularly clever piece is designed to look like a wanted poster. The stickers were also sold in packs of eighteen for twenty-nine cents.

VIEW-MASTER (#B488)			**75**	**64**	**—**

WHISTLE	**Bantam Lite**	**1966**	**40**	**22**	**12**

Another carded toy that made the licensing rounds in the sixties. The oversized plastic whistle has a sketch of the Hornet and Kato on one side and came with a chain for attaching your keys (as if lots of ten-year-old collectors had keys to anything). It is suspected that the whistle may have had a light inside that was activated when squeezed, but don't quote me unless you have one that works at home.

WRIST RADIOS	Remco	1966	200	110	60

Here's that great Remco packaging again. Two four-inch radios came with straps so you could wear them on your wrists, ready for secret communications between the Green Hornet and Kato, right? Yeah, real secret. They worked thanks to a long length of phone wire that had to be attached to each radio. Imagine a bad guy noticing that long wire attached to your wrist. Not too tough, huh? Still, you gotta have it for the package, a nice box with the logo on top and a sketch of our heroes communicating by wrist (no wires shown—so much for truth in packaging).

Here's the inside back page taken from the Gold Key The Green Hornet comic series illustrating the Green Hornet's crime fighting aids. Thank God the Hornet mask protected the Green Hornet's true identity.

THE MAN FROM U.N.C.L.E.

September 1964 - January 1968

It was TV's answer to James Bond. Fast cars, fast action, fast women and every blonde with gun up her sleeve. It was *The Man from U.N.C.L.E.* and in the mid-sixties it was something of a phenomenon. Robert Vaughn began the craze as Napoleon Solo with his dark hair, sly smile and charming wit. He was a secret agent working for the United Network Command for Law and Enforcement. Solo was meant to be a solo act, then along came Illya Kuryakin, the Russian played by Scottish actor David McCallum. Illya was the other side of the seesaw—blonde, baby-faced, the thinker of the group. Between them they captured more female hearts than bad guys. Of course, the bad guys were kind of tough. THRUSH, that equally secret operation devoted to meanness and nastiness, had a penchant for employing curvaceous assassins with vital statistics that would stop a clock.

U.N.C.L.E. was a political parody, but most fans saw it as good clean fun. The dry humor went over the heads of younger audiences, and every boy in town tuned in to see the latest in secret agent hardware. Each week our boys would disappear into that special changing booth in Del Floria's Tailor Shop only to emerge in a huge antiseptic-looking environment with lots of magic sliding doors and more buxom beauties. Heading the organization was Alexander Waverly, played stringently by Leo G. Carroll. He guided our heroes via tiny pen-shaped transmitters that started the world uttering, "Open Channel D." From Venice to Venezuela, Solo and Kuryakin chased spies through every setting imaginable. From backwoods farms to the mountain peaks, from horse races to stock car races—anywhere there was evil, there was a man from U.N.C.L.E.

The show developed a few very recognizable traits that fans still drool over today. Remember the titles, all ending with the word "affair" (i.e. "The Girls from Nazarone Affair")? And after every commercial break a title card would present a new act number and title. Often the sequence of titles were well-written jokes in themselves. *U.N.C.L.E.* writers were known for their parodies of movie and book titles. This inspired plagiarism gave viewers a common starting point for an episode. And who could forget those marvelously dizzying swish transitions between scenes? You know, the ones that look like your VCR is stuck on fast forward. *U.N.C.L.E.*'s creative team wasn't afraid to break the rules and as a result they had one of the most fanciful and delightful series on the air at the time. In 1966, the success of the series prompted the release of a spin-off. When *The Girl From U.N.C.L.E.* premiered, fans could watch two hours of *U.N.C.L.E.* every week. I guess there's just no end to the number of bad guys in the world. Every teenybopper magazine featured Vaughn and McCallum in revealing articles such as "What David Really Likes for Breakfast" and "What Robert Looks for on a Date." Never mind that both men were twice as old as the average reader, they were the stuff dreams were made of.

Heroes, Spies and Medical Men

Now, almost thirty years later, Vaughn still makes TV appearances spoofing his role from *U.N.C.L.E.*, and McCallum can still be found signing photos of Illya after a long career on stage and a stint as TV's Invisible Man. *U.N.C.L.E.* groupies are a solid bunch with fan clubs still active in this and other countries. As a result, *U.N.C.L.E.* toys are quickly snapped up, so arm yourself with your secret cane pistol, tuck your triangle-shaped badge into your jacket pocket, and head out to the local toy show. Above all, beware of shapely blondes bearing gifts. THRUSH will pay anything for a genuine Napoleon Solo doll by Gilbert.

The Man from U.N.C.L.E. Collectibles

			Mint	Ex	Good
BOOK, HARDCOVER	**Whitman**	**1966**	**20**	**15**	**8**

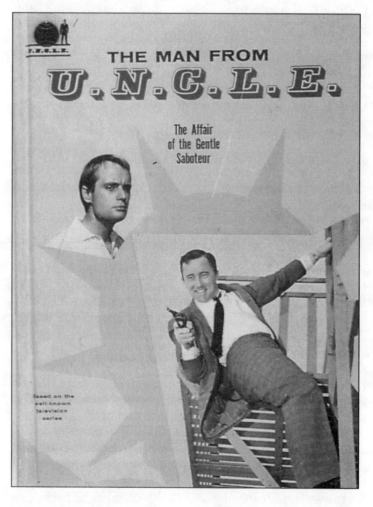

The Man from U.N.C.L.E.: The Affair of the Gentle Saboteur by Brian Keith.

BOOK, HARDCOVER	**Whitman**	**1967**	**20**	**15**	**8**

The Man from U.N.C.L.E.: The Affair of the Gunrunners' Gold.

	Mint	Ex	Good
BOOK, SOFTCOVER **Ace Books** **1965**	—	4.50	—

The Man from U.N.C.L.E. (Ace G-553). The cover states this is "an all-new adventure by Michael Avallone, as U.N.C.L.E.'s top enforcement officer fights a diabolical THRUSH plan for world domination." Look for simply dozens of these at used bookstores and flea markets. A complete set could be worth some money.

	Mint	Ex	Good
CAP FIRING CANE **Marx** **1966**	100	55	30

This aluminum cane came on a cardboard display card. Plastic bullets could be loaded into the handle of the cane and fired with the appropriate cap gun sound effects. I can hear the moms now, "Put that stick down before you put someone's eye out!"

			Mint	Ex	Good
CAR	**Corgi**	**1966**	**125**	**70**	**40**

The "Gun Firing Thrush-Buster" car was a well-detailed metal replica of an Oldsmobile Super 88. Tiny U.N.C.L.E. agents sit in the front seats and they jump out the window if you press a lever on the roof. Nice graphics on the box and Corgi is always a good find.

CAR, DIE CAST	**Playart**	**1968**	**350**	**180**	**90**

A two-and-three-quarter-inch metallic purple die cast metal car.

CARDS, PLAYING	**Ed-U-Cards**	**1965**	**70**	**35**	**15**

Standard fifty-four-card deck with action photo illustrations. Came packaged on a card.

CARDS, PLAYING, BOX	**Ed-U-Cards**	**1965**	**400**	**250**	**125**

This display box holds twelve packs and has a logo and photos.

			Mint	Ex	Good
COLORING BOOK	**Watkins-Strathmore**	**1965**	**50**	**35**	**18**

Contains both "Crush THRUSH Coloring Book" and "The Man from U.N.C.L.E. Coloring Book." 192 pages.

COLORING BOOK	**Whitman**	**1967**	**50**	**35**	**18**

The cover shows Solo and Kuryakin in a winter setting.

COMICS	**Gold Key**	**1965-69**	**30**	**15**	**5**
DOLLS	**AC Gilbert Co.**	**1965**	**150**	**82**	**45**

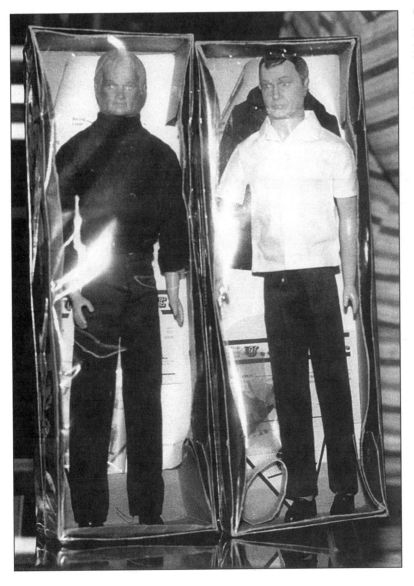

These 12.5-inch action figures tried to capitalize on the GI Joe craze, but I'd say more girls bought them to accompany their Barbies. The figures were modeled after the two stars. The right arm raises to shoot a gun. The dolls came in very unattractive cardboard boxes.

DOLLS (cont.)

	Mint	Ex	Good

DOLL ACCESSORIES	Gilbert	1965	30	17	9

Gilbert made several variations on the accessory pack to go with their dolls. Most of the sets included lots of weapons. Enough to blow away any GI Joe on the block.

			Mint	Ex	Good
FOTO FANTASTIKS	**Eberhard Faber**	**1965**	**75**	**40**	**22**

Here's an attempt to make a violent show more acceptable. This craft kit came from a major craft manufacturer. It features six photo pages, color pencils and a paintbrush. If you colored the photos with the pencils, you could bring the colors to life by going over them with a paintbrush full of water. Magic—just like photos you took yourself. (Yeah, right.)

			Mint	Ex	Good
GAME, BOARD	**Ideal**	**1965**	**40**	**22**	**12**

This game has a nice photo of Solo on the lid with artwork behind. Games rarely command a very big price, even for a popular show like this one.

			Mint	Ex	Good
GAME, CARD	**Milton Bradley**	**1965**	**40**	**22**	**12**

Two more in a series of card games that MB made popular in the era. (Must have been cheaper to make than board games.) Look for the Man from U.N.C.L.E. card game with graphics of Napoleon Solo on the box and the Illya Kuryakin Game with graphics of Illya on the box. Neither will ever take the place of poker.

GUM CARDS	**Topps**	**1966**	**75**	**40**	**22**

Black and white set of fifty-five cards. Each has a nice photo from the show with facsimile autograph. The backs lined up to make a puzzle. The wrapper features a sketch of Solo.

GUN, CIGARETTE LIGHTER	**Ideal**	**1966**	**125**	**70**	**40**

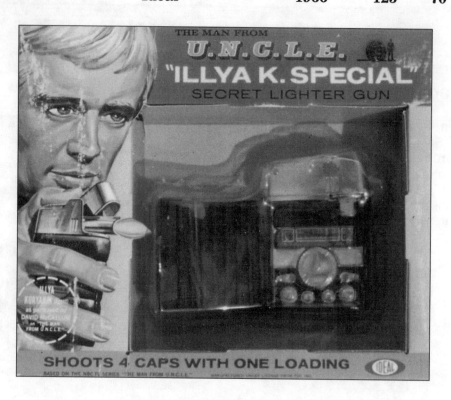

GUN, CIGARETTE LIGHTER (cont.)

One of several "secret weapons" that every good U.N.C.L.E. agent had to possess. This one was a hard plastic lighter with the U.N.C.L.E. logo on the front (so much for SECRET weapon). A gun barrel popped out of the lighter mechanism and a fake radio was housed inside the case. Came in a nice window box with a sketch of Illya on the left side.

				Mint	Ex	Good
GUN SET, SOLO	**Ideal**		1965	600	330	180

GUN SET, SOLO (cont.)

This large play set came with everything a good spy needed to get through a day. The basic pistol could be outfitted with special stock, sights and silencers. The gun fired caps and an U.N.C.L.E. badge and ID card were included. This kit was well marketed in a window box with a nice photo of Robert Vaughn in the lower right corner. This is supposed to be one of the best-selling U.N.C.L.E. toys of the era. That oughta tell you where our minds were in the sixties.

			Mint	Ex	Good
GUN SET, ILLYA	**Ideal**	1965	200	110	60

Not nearly as impressive as Solo's set. Illya only gets a souped up handgun with a clip for bullets, and a badge. I guess Illya is a better shot than his partner.

			Mint	Ex	Good

GUN SET, SECRET SERVICE   Ideal   1965   350   195   105

Solo is solo on this box with a single black plastic pistol, holster and badge set. Question: Since when is Napoleon Solo a member of the Secret Service?

GUN SET, SECRET WEAPONS   Ideal   1965   350   195   105

Ideal knew a good thing when they had it. This version came with a pistol, holster and several grenades for your enjoyment. None of these brutal-looking weapons look very secret, but what's in a name?

GUN, THRUSH RIFLE   Ideal   1966   1000   550   300

Hey, the bad guys have to be armed too! If they weren't, you couldn't use all those other cool weapons that Ideal had out on the market. This large plastic rifle was customized with a futuristic scope on the top. When you looked in the sight you saw the targets. When you pulled the trigger, the targets would disappear. Could be worse. Could have been Illya in there.

LUNCH BOX   King Seeley   1966   200   110   60

LUNCH BOX (cont.)

This metal lunch box came trimmed in yellow with action graphics on all sides. Unfortunately, the artwork is terribly cartoonish and Illya has a tendency to look like Alfred E. Newman. Not surprising, since the illustration was done by *MAD* magazine artist Jack Davis. It's colorful, but just a bit too fun.

			Mint	Ex	Good
MODEL, CAR	AMT	1967	125	70	40

This 1:24 scale kit is a rare find but it still does not command the price an Aurora kit gets. It is a replica of the sporty U.N.C.L.E. car with the doors that open upward like wings. The 9" x 15" box is close to ugly, which is probably why it's rare—nobody noticed it.

			Mint	Ex	Good
MODEL, FIGURES	Aurora	1966	500	275	150

Aurora had two more winners with these 13" x 4" boxed figure kits. Each U.N.C.L.E. agent could be built separately, but if you had them both they interlocked to make a diorama. (Cool.) Napoleon is featured jumping over a short brick wall, gun in hand. Illya can be found crouched behind a gatepost next to the wall. Both are clutching vicious looking U.N.C.L.E. weapons and have a small plaque at the base of the kit. The box art isn't up to Aurora's usual standard and the figures' resemblance to the actors is minimal, but the connectability of the two kits makes it a fun find. Price is for each.

			Mint	Ex	Good
PINBALL GAME	**Marx**	1966	125	70	40

This tabletop pinball style game came with a secret code wheel in the center. The wheel contained small bubble gum machine type prizes that you could "win" if you shot all of the pinballs into the correct keys. Marx had done very well with its "Electro Shot Shooting Gallery," and this game was a nice variation on that theme.

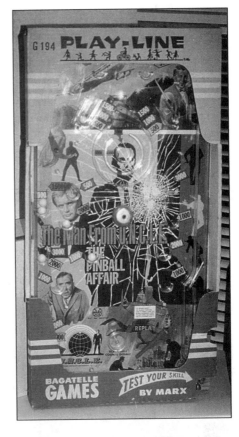

			Mint	Ex	Good
PRINT PUTTY	**Colorforms**	1965	75	40	15

Basically, silly putty in a gun-shaped container. Came with print paper, display cards of Kuryakin and Solo, and a book of spy and weapons illustrations. Packaged on a card.

			Mint	Ex	Good
PUPPET, ILLYA KURYAKIN	**Gilbert**	1965	350	225	100

A thirteen-inch soft vinyl hand puppet of Illya holding a communicator. Came on a 10" x 16" card.

			Mint	Ex	Good
PUPPETS, FINGER	**Dean**	1966	550	300	150

Six vinyl characters: THRUSH agent, Solo, Kuryakin, Waverly, and two female agents. Came in a die cut window box. Box contained cutouts for props.

			Mint	Ex	Good
PUZZLE	**Milton Bradley**	1966	65	40	20

"Illya's Battle Below." 10" x 19", one hundred pieces.

			Mint	Ex	Good
PUZZLE	**Milton Bradley**	**1966**	**65**	**40**	**20**

"Illya Crushes THRUSH." 10" x 19", one hundred pieces.

PUZZLES	**Milton Bradley**	**1965**	**65**	**40**	**25**

The Mystery Jigsaw Puzzles Series included "The Loyal Groom," "The Vital Observation," "The Impossible Escape," and "The Microfilm Affair." Puzzles were 14" x 24", 250 pieces, and came with a story booklet. Price is for each.

PUZZLES	**England**	**1966**	**160**	**100**	**45**

Four different puzzles: "The Getaway," "Solo in Trouble," "The Frogman Affair," and "Secret Plans." 11" x 17", 340 pieces. Price is for each.

SECRET MESSAGE PEN	**American Character**	**1966**	**300**	**180**	**90**

A six-and-one-half-inch double-tipped pen for writing invisible messages. Came on a header card.

SPY MAGIC TRICKS	**Gilbert**	**1965**	**475**	**300**	**150**

This photo boxed set contains a mystery gun, Illya playing cards, and many tricks and items.

SWEATER	**Brentwood**	**1965**	**300**	**180**	**90**

One hundred percent acrylic sweater with the U.N.C.L.E. logo on neck tag.

		Mint	Ex	Good
VIEW-MASTER	**Sawyers/ View-Master**	1966	60	40	20

A three-reel set and storybook from "The Very Important Zombie Affair."

	Mint	Ex	Good
VIEW-MASTER (#B484)	28	24	—

Not even the cover shot is exciting on this one, but if you're collecting, you gotta have it.

WATCH	**Bradley**	1966	425	275	130

The Secret Agent Watch had a gray face showing Solo holding a communicator. The watch came in a case and had either a plain "leather" or "mod" watch band.

BATMAN

January 1966 - March 1968

"Atomic batteries to power, turbines to speed, ready—move out." Insert cool music here and we're off on a flight of fun and fancy with famous guest stars in roles the likes of which television has never seen before. Holy Hit Series! It's *Batman*! In 1939, The Bat-Man made his first appearance in the May issue of *Detective Comics*. His creator Bob Kane could never have imagined where his character would go. Adam West went from a fairly slow-moving acting career to the cover of *Life* magazine when he assumed the role as Bruce Wayne, alias Batman. At his side was Bruce's ward, Dick Grayson, aka Robin the Boy Wonder, played by Burt Ward. Burt, who was only nineteen at the time, joined the cast with no professional acting credits to his name. (Little known bat fact: Burt used to practice his martial arts with his neighbor, another would-be star, Bruce Lee.) Also residing at stately Wayne Manor was Alfred the butler, played with great aplomb by Alan Napier, and Dick's great-aunt Harriet Cooper, overacted by Madge Blake. Also appearing each week were Stafford Repp as Chief O'Hara and Neil Hamilton as Commissioner Gordon. Neither were capable of handling crime in the city without the help of the Caped Crusaders.

When *Batman* hit the small screen, it wasn't exactly what comic fans had in mind. Instead of the dark, brooding, serious crime serial they were used to, fans were greeted with blasts of bright color, an abundance of hammy acting and writing that was so corny it was brilliant. Everything in Gotham City was just a half bubble off the real world. Like the rest of the Bat world, the villains of *Batman* were more than just a little off, they were cosmic! Julie Newmar as the Catwoman in her painted on cat suit; Frank Gorshin all in green as the Riddler; Caesar Romero as the pasty-faced Joker. There came a time when being a guest villain on *Batman* was the hottest job in Hollywood. Boy, did the stars come out. Roddy McDowell as the Bookworm, Vincent Price as Egghead, and Victor Buono as King Tut. Enough, you say. Not nearly, there were Zsa Zsa Gabor, Joan Collins, Carolyn Jones, John Astin, and Cliff Robertson. Not only was Hollywood caught red-handed, but the music biz soon joined in with visits from Leslie Gore, Chad and Jeremy, and Paul Revere and The Raiders. *Batman* was hip, cool, like-crazy man, from its pun-ridden cliffhangers to the Zap!, POW! fight sounds on the screen. For a year and a half the series aired in two parts, with slots on Wednesday and Thursday, an unusual idea then and now. By 1967, the show was in need of a lift, which came in the form of Yvonne Craig as Batgirl. In make-believe real life, Batgirl was Barbara Gordon, daughter to Commissioner Gordon and head librarian for Gotham Library. In a suit that bore a striking resemblance to Catwoman, Batgirl turned the Dynamic Duo into the Terrific Trio. (And she could kick better than any Kung Fu master I've ever seen.) The new blood helped ratings for awhile, but it was an uphill battle. The show changed its format in 1968, going to half an hour once a week. Gone were the great cliffhangers and most of the great villains. The last few episodes of the series were painfully poor with villains like Milton Berle as Louie the Lilac. And who can ever remember Ida Lupino as Dr. Cassandra Spellcraft?

Given the popularity of the series, one would think *Batman* would be the most licensed TV show of the era. WRONG. Actually, the opposite is true. The faces of Ward and West were never used on a toy. All of the items produced during the run of the series were done with sketches that resembled Bob Kane's comics. It would seem someone had an aversion to seeing the actors get a piece of the licensing pie. For the purpose of this book, *Batman* TV collectibles are defined as any toy produced from 1966 to 1967.

Batman Collectibles

			Mint	Ex	Good
ART KIT	Hasbro	1966	75	42	22

Hasbro produced an oil paint-by-number set and a colored pencil set. Box artwork is unusually nice.

			Mint	Ex	Good
BATBIKE	Corgi		100	60	40

Has a four-and-one-quarter-inch black one-piece plastic body, black and red plastic parts, gold engine and exhaust pipes, clear windshield, and black plastic spoked wheels. Includes a Batman figure and decals.

			Mint	Ex	Good
BATCOPTER	Corgi		75	40	25

Corgi also made a helicopter with a five-and-one-half-inch black body; yellow, red, and black decals; and red rotors. Includes a Batman figure.

			Mint	Ex	Good
CAVE TUN-L	New York Toy	1966	2000	1550	1250

Hours of fun for any Bat-child, this tunnel consists of two spring steel hoops with a bright cloth covering. The tunnel stretches to over ten feet long and is two feet in diameter. The cloth covering had five-color illustrations. Came in a 26" x 26" x 2" box.

			Mint	Ex	Good
COINS	Transogram	1966	50	27	15

Early version of POG it seems. This was a pack of plastic coins with pictures of the characters on them. The set came shrink-wrapped to a card.

			Mint	Ex	Good
COLORING BOOK	Watkins-Strathmore	1966	75	60	50

The "Robin Strikes for Batman" coloring book contains illustrations from the Batman comics.

			Mint	Ex	Good
COLORING BOOK	**Whitman**	**1966**	**30**	**17**	**9**

Whitman released two different coloring books and one sticker book in 1966. All have covers that look more like the comic than the show.

			Mint	Ex	Good
COMIC BOOK, 3-D	**DC Comics**	**1966**	**30**	**25**	**20**

A 9" x 11" comic with 3-D pages and those oh-so-cool 3-D glasses.

			Mint	Ex	Good
FIGURE, BATMAN	**Ideal**	**1966**	**20**	**15**	**10**

This three-inch yellow plastic figure came with a detachable gray plastic cape.

			Mint	Ex	Good
FLYING COPTER	**Remco**	**1966**	**100**	**55**	**30**

Remco doing its usual—a plain plastic helicopter with a guide wire outfitted with Batman stickers and packed in a box with the comic face of Batman in the corner.

			Mint	Ex	Good
GAME, BOARD	**Hasbro**	**1965**	**50**	**27**	**15**

"Help Batman and Robin capture the Joker" was the subtitle on this board game by Hasbro.

			Mint	Ex	Good
GAME, BOARD	**Milton Bradley**	**1966**	**55**	**45**	**35**

This Batman board game by MB game with four playing pieces, a board, and character cards.

			Mint	Ex	Good
GAME, TARGET	**Hasbro**	**1966**	**85**	**75**	**60**

A tin litho target with a plastic revolver and rubber-tipped darts.

			Mint	Ex	Good
GUM CARDS	**Topps**	**1966**	**70**	**38**	**21**

There are five different sets of bubble gum cards, all of which were made by Topps in 1966. Batman, the A Series, and the B Series are all comic book style sketches with captions or puzzles on the back. The cards are numbered and lettered so it is easy to match a set. After all that, Topps released two sets of photo cards. One is called the Riddler Back set, since each photo has a Riddler style word game on the back. The photos are framed with corner mounts so they look like photos in an old-fashioned album. The last set features photos with a very small white border and Bat Laffs on the back. This last series is the only one to use a photo of the actors on the wrappers. One of those wrappers would sell for $50 and up, a little less for the cartoon wrappers. A clean empty box goes for $75 to $100.

	Mint	Ex	Good

LUNCH BOX **Aladdin** **1966** **150** **82** **45**

Another Elmer Lenhardt winner. The box, which is square metal and trimmed in black, has a very nice sketch of Batman and Robin beating up a normal looking bad guy. Rumor has it Aladdin didn't want the rights to the box because they thought the show was dumb. So dumb the box sold millions!!

MAGIC RUB OFFS **Whitman** **1966** **40** **22** **12**

This was a box of slick pictures with wax crayons that could be wiped off after coloring. Box features a tight sketch of Batman with Robin in the background.

MODEL, BATMAN **Aurora** **1964** **400** **220** **120**

Extremely accurate figure of Batman leaping into action with his Batarang. The base came with an old tree and a stump with several bats and an owl. When properly painted, Batman's cape looks like it's billowing in the breeze. The kit was re-released in the seventies without the owl and in a different box. The reissue sells for less than half the going price.

MODEL, BATMOBILE **Aurora** **1966** **300** **165** **90**

The Batmobile was one of Aurora's biggest sellers. It came in two different boxes, light blue and purple. The purple box is harder to find. The box art is not particularly thrilling, but the car detail is good.

			Mint	Ex	Good
MODEL, BATPLANE	**Aurora**	**1967**	**250**	**200**	**75**

Aurora's 1:60 scale, plastic Batplane kit included a decal sheet, a display stand, and figures of Batman and Robin.

			Mint	Ex	Good
MODEL, ROBIN	**Aurora**	**1966**	**200**	**110**	**60**

The Robin kit is another fine action pose, cape billowing once more. Robin is tripping over lab equipment to get to a switch marked "Stop" on an electronic machine of some sort. The face of the figure is ghastly and he's a bit pudgy in the middle, but the setting is fun. The original box showed a clean comic book style sketch of The Boy Wonder. The 1974 reissue has a darker, jazzed up box and, voilà, he's now The Teen Wonder. Rumor has it a large stock of the original model was found in a warehouse in the eighties, causing the price of the kit to drop. By the turn of the century it ought to be right back up there again.

			Mint	Ex	Good
PAJAMAS	**Wormser**	**1966**	**900**	**750**	**600**

Light blue, two-piece child's pajamas with a full-color Batman logo on the chest.

			Mint	Ex	Good
PHONE	**Marx**	**1966**	**200**	**110**	**60**

The Batman Hot Line was an eight-inch red plastic phone. It was battery operated and would say ten different phrases when you picked up the receiver. There were several Bat stickers on the phone and a nice flip top display box.

			Mint	Ex	Good
PICTURE PISTOL	Marx	1966	400	220	120

This was a "Give-a-Show" projector disguised as a gun. Extremely strange since Batman didn't carry any kind of gun. This overgrown pistol came with three small films that could be projected on the wall. The gun is oddly shaped and has the *Batman* logo on the handle.

PLAY SET	Ideal	1966	900	500	270

This set was designed by Ideal and sold as a Sears Christmas exclusive, although it wasn't really exclusive, since it was marketed in a different box by other stores. The set included plastic buildings, panels and scenery, including an entrance to the Bat-cave marked "SANCTUARY." Obviously the kit was designed with the comic in mind, since the figures included Batman, Robin, the Joker, Kaltor, and Mouse Man. (Mouse Man? Didn't Paul Williams play that part?) The Sears set came in a plain cardboard box; everywhere else it was in a display box.

PLAY SET, MAGIC MAGNETIC	Remco	1966	800	440	240

Here's a one-of-a-kind toy. A table with Gotham City re-created in cardboard along with assorted figures and vehicles to play inside. A heavy duty magnet wand came with the set. You were supposed to run the magnet under the table to make the people and cars move by magic. Of course, if you wanted to have an effective fight scene, you'd need three friends and five more magnets. What will they think of next?

PUPPETS	Ideal	1966	100	55	30

These hand puppets came with soft vinyl heads and plastic glove style bodies with their figures painted on the front. Look for Robin, Batman, and the Joker. Highest price goes to the Duo packaged together in a nicely designed window box. Loose, the puppets sell for $40-$50.

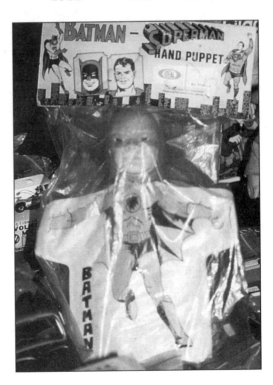

Heroes, Spies and Medical Men

			Mint	Ex	Good
PUPPET THEATRE	**Ideal**	**1966**	**400**	**220**	**120**

Another Sears exclusive. Cardboard puppet stage came with all three puppets. Pretty rare.

			Mint	Ex	Good
PUZZLE, FRAME	**Whitman**	**1966**	**210**	**200**	**185**

This jigsaw puzzle in an 11" x 14" frame tray depicts Batman and Robin thwarting the Joker.

			Mint	Ex	Good
RECORD SET	**Golden Records**	**1966**	**100**	**50**	**25**

This Batman set included the original story comic magazine, an LP record, an official club membership card and button, PLUS a needlecraft framed picture!

			Mint	Ex	Good
RECORD, SOUNDTRACK	**20th Century Fox**	**1966**	**250**	**225**	**210**

The stereo version of the *Batman* soundtrack sported a cover shot of West and Ward in the Batmobile.

			Mint	Ex	Good
RECORD, SOUNDTRACK	**20th Century Fox**	**1966**	**220**	**210**	**195**

Mono version of the above.

			Mint	Ex	Good
SLOT CAR	**Magicar**	**1966**	**325**	**210**	**115**

This English car was a five-inch Batmobile being driven by Batman and Robin. It came in an illustrated display window box.

SOAKYS	**Colgate-Palmolive**	**1966**	**75**	**40**	**22**

Soaky was a bubble bath that came in plastic figural containers. Batman and Robin were both immortalized for the bath with overblown heads and out of proportion bodies. "To the bathtub, Robin!"

SWITCH AND GO	**Mattel**	**1966**	**400**	**220**	**120**

Mattel got a lot of mileage out of this toy, which was basically a racetrack customized to suit various TV shows. This set included a nice Batmobile, which was powered by an air pump, and small figures of the villains for you to run over.

TRACE-A-GRAPH	**Emenee**	**1966**	**125**	**70**	**40**

Another generic toy with good packaging. This kit was basically a light table with a Batman logo at the top. The kit came with several darkline drawings that could be put under the light table and traced to give you the feel of being a real artist. (I wonder if Disney does it this way.)

UTILITY BELT	**Ideal**	**1966**	**1000**	**550**	**300**

What no Batfan should be without: your own private utility belt complete with Bat-arang, hand-cuffs, flashlight, Bat pistol, radio, rope, grappling hook and grenades. To quote the box, "A complete set of crime fighting equipment" with an adjustable belt that fits all sizes up to thirty-two-inch waist.

	Mint	Ex	Good
VIEW-MASTER REELS	**3-15**	**2-13**	**—**

Several reels were released over the years. They included The Animated Series (3086), Batman Returns (4137), The Joker's Wild (1003), The Perfect Crime (4011), and several simply titled Batman (B4792, BB492, 1086).

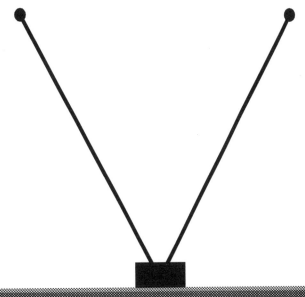

CALL TO ARMS:

WAR ON
TELEVISION

When George M. Cohan put pen to paper and wrote "Over There," he was adding to the image that soldiering was an honorable profession. You remember those old movies where the moms and dads smile proudly as their son shoulders his rifle. And the parades! A brass band was always around to greet the first wave when they arrived home. Our image of war used to be a patriotic one—red, white and blue, and Uncle Sam. Doing what you can for the war effort, growing a victory garden, and saving rubber for tank tires. Somewhere between World War II and Vietnam, that image went up in smoke. Not the proverbial bombs bursting in air; more like a land mine in the middle of a country road.

In the early 1960s, families gathered to watch *The Rat Patrol* or *Twelve O'Clock High*. Even though there was death and destruction, it was still considered wholesome entertainment for the family. Fathers saw themselves in the hardworking heroes, and children wished to be just like them. Imagine piloting a fighter plane, shooting down the enemy, or driving a tank right into a Nazi stronghold. Even girls were plied with images of female spies stealing secrets for God and country, or nurses putting their lives on the line to save the men of the 101st. In the sixties, we thought what we were doing was right, and we encouraged it with the toys we put in our children's hands. Automatic weapons, walkie-talkies, jeeps and tanks. Bazookas that "really work" and hand grenades that look "just like the real thing." Don't forget the toy company that marketed Johnny Reb, the replica Civil War cannon. GI Joe would be proud. War was a big seller.

In the late sixties, war went from honorable to horrible. In the wake of the assassination of two Kennedys and civil rights leader Martin Luther King, parents began to rethink the idea of putting toy guns in the hands of their children. Protest groups squawked loudly over the amount of violence on TV and suddenly the shows we had loved were marked as "glorifying war." Soon we didn't need make-believe war on TV; we had the real thing. Instead of watching Sgt. Troy blow up an ammo dump in the desert, we could watch Jimmy Jones from next door being pulled from the smoking wreckage of a plane. With the Vietnam War airing on every station, viewers got a good look at what war was all about and it turned their stomachs. Before this time, an outbreak of war had done a lot to boost war toy sales. For the first time in history, the opposite was true. Vietnam sent parents clamoring for innocent toys, dolls and crafts, and Hot Wheels cars. The military market hit an all-time low and war shows were canceled, replaced by silly comedies.

Now, some twenty years later, we are able to put things in perspective again. The wars are over for now and GI Joe is a big seller again. Now we can look back at the toys of our youth and see them for what they were: not tools for make-believe destruction, but symbols of the fight for American freedom.

TWELVE O'CLOCK HIGH

September 1964 - January 1967

It was *Combat* in the air. Realistic, gritty, "let's win this one for the folks back home" kind of TV drama. It was *Twelve O'Clock High*, based on the movie starring Gregory Peck. The television series was produced by Quinn Martin, who had already made quite a name for himself as a TV genius after launching *The Fugitive* and *The Untouchables*. Martin hopped on the war bandwagon with this story of an Air Corps bombardment group based near London during World War II. Originally, the series starred veteran leading man Robert Lansing as Brigadier General Frank Savage. Unlike most war shows of the time, the officers in this group spent more time in the trenches than behind a desk. Savage led every bombing mission personally. He was backed up by Major Harvey Stoval, played by Frank Overton; Major Joe Cobb, played by Lew Gallo; and Major General Wiley Crowe, played by John Larkin.

It was a cursed group. Larkin died suddenly during the run of the series, Overton never had another series after *TOH*, and Gallo and Lansing were cut from the show after the first season. The story goes, Lansing had his own ideas about the direction the series should take. Producer Quinn Martin didn't take very kindly to the suggestions and to make his point he did something unprecedented—he killed off the lead character of a successful TV show. General Savage was shot down by a German in a phony B-17 bomber at the beginning of the second season. It was quite a blow to Lansing and to fans of the series. The printed version of what happened played a little differently. The studio reported Lansing was being replaced by a younger actor in hopes of appealing to a younger audience when the show made its move to an earlier time slot. This move was also odd. As a matter of fact, *Twelve O'Clock High* had one of the oddest airing histories ever. In less than two years, the series went from Fridays at 9:30 to Fridays at 10:00, to Mondays at 7:30, back to Fridays at 10:00. So much for the new younger audience appeal. Not that it really mattered, since thirty-seven-year-old Lansing was replaced by thirty-nine-year-old Paul Burke. Burke was cast in the role of Col. Joe Gallagher, a man plagued by guilty feelings due to the death of his friend Savage. Although Burke is relatively unknown today, at the time he was quite a hot property. He had turned down offers to do sixteen other series before he accepted the role on *Twelve O'Clock High* and he only did so because he wanted to work for Quinn Martin. Filling out the second season cast was Tech Sgt. Sandy Komansky, played by *General Hospital* star Chris Robinson, and Brigadier Gen. Ed Britt, played by Andrew Duggan.

Ironically, Paul Burke had appeared in the very first episode of the series as a different Capt. Gallagher. The story surrounds Gallagher's need for special treatment since his father was a military hotshot. In this episode, Lansing chews him up one side and down the other, calling him a disgrace to the uniform, saying, "I am going to be your worst enemy." It would seem that prophecy came true. In the end, the change of cast didn't really seem to matter at all. The stories were still the same, generally people-oriented, focusing on the human frailties that often rear their ugly heads during a war. But check out these synopses from *TV Guide*: "Follow the Leader": "To improve bombing techniques, Savage has the whole group depend on the accuracy of the leader." "Back to the Drawing Board": "Gallagher is given the top secret assignment of evaluating a primitive air-borne radar for bombing through cloud cover." Hmm, kind of hard to tell the players without a score card, isn't it?

Twelve O'Clock High Collectibles

			Mint	Ex	Good
COMICS	**Dell**	**1965**	**30**	**15**	**4**

Dell only released two issues of the comic for this series. Not surprising, since the show's 10:00 time slot is way past the bedtime of most comic book readers.

GAME, BOARD	**Ideal**	**1965**	**50**	**27**	**15**

The object here is to blow away the most enemy soldiers on the ground. The board shows a German landscape and lots of bomb cards to release on it. The lid of this game was originally released with a picture of Robert Lansing and the logo superimposed over an air battle in progress. When Lansing was canned from the series, Ideal re-released the game with a photo of Paul Burke on the cover. While the Lansing issue is more difficult to find, neither one commands a higher price.

GAME, CARD	**Milton Bradley**	**1965**	**30**	**17**	**9**

Another of MB's oversized card games. The box art is particularly unattractive with a tight shot from the point of view of an airplane gunner blowing the enemy out of the sky.

PUZZLE	**Milton Bradley**	**1965**	**30**	**17**	**9**

This hundred-piece Junior Jigsaw Puzzle is a depiction of the squadron in flight, and of course, the bombs are dropping.

THE RAT PATROL

September 1966 - September 1968

Two heavily armed jeeps hurl themselves over a sand dune straight into your television screen. Leapin' Jeeps! It's *The Rat Patrol*. Set in the deserts of Africa, *The Rat Patrol* followed the exploits of a long-range desert patrol. Christopher George played Sgt. Sam Troy, leader of the rats in his rakish Australian bush hat. British actor Gary Raymond played the next in command, Sgt. Jack Moffitt, resident translator and archaeologist often seen wearing the hat of the British Scots Grays. Driving for Troy was Lawrence Casey as the Ivy League Private, Mark Hitchcock, complete with wire-rimmed glasses and a French Foreign Legion cap. Justin Tarr was Moffitt's right-hand man in the character of Kentucky ridge runner Tully Pettigrew, the only one of the bunch to wear a regulation army helmet.

For two years, the patrol ran around behind enemy lines confounding their regular enemy, Captain Hans Dietrich, played admirably by now famous soap star Eric Braedon (aka Hans Gudegast). Each week, our heroes would shoot, bomb, and shell the enemy, always defeating at least a dozen German soldiers. Unlike most war dramas of the time, *The Rat Patrol* was a half hour series. This time constraint forced the show to be long on action and short on characterization. Even so, episodes of *The Rat Patrol* are populated with a long list of veteran TV actors. Ed Asner puts in an appearance as a German doctor torn between his oath as a man of medicine and his oath as an officer of the Reich. Gavin McLeod turns out a fine performance as a truly despicable soldier whose only goal in life is the saving of his own butt. Even teen heartthrobs Fabian and Jack Jones had episodes written to suit their various talents.

TV audiences loved *The Rat Patrol*, and they made it the only new show of the season to premiere in the top ten, beating out its competition, *The Lucy Show*. Unfortunately, no amount of audience praise could save *The Rat Patrol* from the critics. The show was often criticized for its lack of realism and overabundance of violence. In the end, it was the violent content that knocked it off the air when the country began its rally against guns in the wake of two major assassinations in one year (presidential hopeful Robert Kennedy and civil rights leader Martin Luther King).

Violent content or not, toy manufacturers made a mint on the *Rat Patrol* license. *The Rat Patrol* spawned more toys than any other war show on TV. The most collectible are the action play sets, which bore a strong resemblance to the GI Joe line of toys. Marketers at the time had no fear of promoting the violent image. They had come from an era in which the soldier was revered. And so the play set came equipped with grenade launchers "that really worked" and the *Rat Patrol* coloring book even carried the *Parents* magazine seal of approval. It was definitely the end of an era.

Rat Patrol Collectibles

			Mint	Ex	Good
COLORING BOOK	**Saalfield**	**1966**	**40**	**22**	**12**

This eight-page coloring book sold for ten cents and actually bears a seal that reads "commended by Parents Magazine." (Can you imagine *The Terminator* commended by *Highlights for Children?*)

COMICS	**Dell**	**1967**	**30**	**15**	**4**

Six comics were produced with number six being a reprint of number one. All have great photo covers and story lines that took more thought than the series' scripts.

COSTUME	**Ben Cooper**	**1967**	**100**	**55**	**30**

You could be the leader of the pack in this Halloween costume. The typical polyester jumpsuit came in desert tan with a mask depicting Troy and his bush hat.

DOLL	**Marx**	**1967**	**125**	**70**	**40**

To coincide with the release of their play set, Marx test marketed individually carded dolls to add to the set, which came with only two figures. The Jack Moffit doll came shrink-wrapped to a card along with a few accessories. The ad copy on the toy read, "Fully jointed - can be put in 100 different positions." Five of these positions are illustrated, leaving the other ninety-five to your imagination.

			Mint	Ex	Good
GAME	**Pressman**	**1967**	**100**	**55**	**30**

Pressman produced a Spin to Win Game which was part of a long line of TV tie-in Spin to Wins. The game came in a 15" x 12" box with nice graphics of Troy behind the 50mm jeep-mounted gun. As games go, this one is fairly rare.

GAME, BOARD	**Transogram**	**1967**	**75**	**40**	**22**

The Rat Patrol Desert Combat Game is a board game with similar graphics on the box. Even though it's nothing special, it's hard to find, suggesting that not very many were made. As a result, the price is usually higher than most board games of the era.

GUM CARDS	**Topps**	**1966**	**125**	**70**	**40**

Set of sixty-six color photo cards with puzzle pieces on the backs. Each pack came with one of twenty-two cardboard Army Insignia rings. Since the rings were generally punched out and worn by the buyers, finding a set of rings intact is a real challenge. A complete set of cards will run you $100, more if you can find a wrapper or a box.

JEEP	**Remco**	**1967**	**75**	**40**	**22**

For collectors with less space, Remco had the Midget Motors Jeep. This six-inch hard plastic jeep was outfitted with logo stickers on the side and classic machine gun mount on the back. The toy was designed to make realistic engine noises as it ran over the dunes in your backyard sandbox.

LUNCH BOX	**Aladdin**	**1967**	**65**	**35**	**20**

LUNCH BOX (cont.)

Nice artwork garnishes all sides of this embossed metal lunch box. See the boys leap! See them shoot! See them blow up the bad guys!!!

			Mint	Ex	Good
MODEL	Aurora	1967	125	70	40

The Rat Patrol Diorama. The model box is 25" x 10" x 15" and features a very striking painting of the rat patrol in the midst of battle. The actual diorama consists of two small jeeps, tanks, and an overabundance of palm trees. Forget the model; display the box.

PLAY SET	Marx	1967	1200	660	360

Marx turned out a fantastically detailed play set for Sears. This Christmas exclusive was only produced in limited quantities, making it one of the toughest collectibles to obtain. The set came with a large jeep and an assortment of accessories such as walkie-talkies, rifles, ammo bags, and so on. Included were two GI Joe-sized dolls dressed in desert tan. One doll does look like Christopher George, while the other tends to resemble Gary Raymond. No matter though, because the set provided you with all four distinctive hats, so you could make any combination of two characters.

			Mint	Ex	Good
PLAY SET	**Remco**	**1967**	**200**	**110**	**60**

Remco also released a play set that should cost you a little less at the next toy show. The Rat Patrol Action Battle Set has a box straight out of the sixties with phrases like "everything really works" and "based on the exciting ABC TV series" plastered all over it. The box art shows a few photos from the show with a delightful caricature of the group in one corner. The set itself

is less impressive than the box. The toys were nothing more than Remco's basic World War II vehicle set remolded in desert tan. The set includes one jeep, one tank, two ammo carriers, and one grenade launcher that "really works." You could shoot your friends to your heart's content.

COMBAT

October 1962 - August 1967

It was the first war show of the sixties. It was also the longest running war show of the sixties. It was down to earth. It was dark. It was gritty. It was *Combat*. Set in Europe during World War II, *Combat* followed the foot soldiers, the men who fought the war up close and personal. Rick Jason, a man never heard from again, starred as Lt. Gil Hanley. Quickly upstaging Jason was a new rising star named Vic Morrow as Sgt. Chip Saunders. Morrow had that tough-on-the-outside look with the I'd-lay-it-all-on-the-line for-my-men kind of heart. He led his troops asking nothing he wouldn't do himself, and with his five o'clock shadow and cool dark eyes, he earned a place in the hearts of young girls everywhere.

Combat was a busy show with lots of action and heavy emphasis on newsreel footage. The show was a bit character-heavy with a long list of regulars. Pierre Jalbert played the cocky Cajun, Caje (shades of Gambit from the X-Men). Jalbert was the only actor besides the leads to last the entire run of the series. Comic actor Shecky Greene left the show in 1963, as did Steven Rogers, who had played Doc Walton. With the start of the 1963 season, the *Combat* cast grew with the addition of Jack Hogan as the all-American, Kirby. Dick Peabody played a giant called Littlejohn and Conlon Carter came in as the new Doc.

Although *Combat* is credited as the show that started them all, its look is distinctly different from *The Rat Patrol* or *Garrison's Gorillas*. *Combat* always had a weary look about it. The men were constantly filthy and tired. The plots were often disheartening. Some stories were action based: getting through a minefield, alluding capture, surviving the elements. Others were people based: the newbie who thinks the world owes him a living, the orphaned children who need a home, the cost of a man's first kill. The best moments can be found in the camaraderie of the men and their efforts to stay sane in a world that is blowing up around them. *Combat* is as close as you get to watching a documentary on World War II. Next time you flip through the *TV Guide* look out for a two-parter called "The Long Road Home." It stars Richard Basehart as a Nazi SS officer. This particularly moody episode deals with Morrow trying to help his men escape from a prison camp as Basehart begins his reign of terror upon them. The villains of *Combat* are rarely played as stereotypes and are never played as stupid. It is quite the opposite in this episode, as we see one of the good guys played as a coward while the bad guys hold all the cards. It is a striking, breath-stealing, Hitchcockian story that will leave you anxiously awaiting next week.

Even though the series was aimed at adults, *Combat* was well-licensed in the toy department. Generic war toys—guns, tanks, and military strategy games—soon bore pictures of Morrow and Jason. In no time at all, every kid in America could be found marching through the muddy fields in his own backyard, M-16 in hand, grenades on his belt, whistling that happy little theme.

Combat Collectibles

			Mint	Ex	Good
COLORING BOOK	**Saalfield**	1963	40	22	12

More mayhem to color. Red for blood, black for smoke, gray for tanks....

GAME, BOARD	**Ideal**	1963	100	55	30

The "Combat at Anzio Beach" game in an oversized cardboard envelope. There are photos of Rick Jason and Vic Morrow on the front. Because the packaging was so easily torn, this game is much more valuable than most games from the era.

GAME, BOARD	**Ideal**	1963	75	40	22

This one is called "The Combat Fighting Infantry Game" and is completely different from Ideal's other version. This box has a very dark action shot of Morrow and Jason on the lid while all heck is breaking loose behind them.

GAME, CARD	**Milton Bradley**	1964	50	27	15

Milton Bradley had a lot of those giant cards around so they made another card game. This one has a nice sketch of the men in action on the cover.

GUM CARDS	**Donruss**	1963	100	55	30

Donruss made two series of cards, totaling 132. The fronts have black and white photos from the show. Descriptions are on the back. The cards are marked Series I and Series II. Oddly, the two wrappers are identical except that one identifies the men as Lt. Hanley and Sgt. Saunders, while the other identifies the actors as Rick Jason and Vic Morrow. The box has a very poorly drawn sketch of the two actors. Since the death of actor Vic Morrow, cards bearing his likeness are slightly more collectible. P.S. Check out some of the card titles like: #50, Die American; and #35, An Anxious Prisoner.

			Mint	Ex	Good
PAINT SET	**Hasbro**	**1963**	**125**	**70**	**40**

Hasbro made two versions of the oil paint set. One came in a carry case with three sketches and paints. The front shows an American tank and two gunners taking out one German soldier. The other set came in a box with the proclamation, "You can paint a picture like this" below a charming scene of soldiers landing on Anzio Beach.

PLAY SET	**Diamond**	**1963**	**200**	**110**	**60**

The Combat Battle Gear Set is one of the most sought after pieces. It was a set of military armaments: full-size machine gun, pistol, knife, grenade, and a weapons belt for holding it all. Just imagine, you could kill your friends in four different ways.

PLAY SET	**Diamond**	**1963**	**300**	**165**	**90**

The Official Combat Set was like the gear set with a few added survival features, such as a canteen and binoculars. It came in a box.

PLAY SET	**Superior Toys**	**1963**	**250**	**140**	**75**

This play set is the action figure type. Seventy-two pieces include a whole company of jeeps, trucks, soldiers and ammunition. Probably a generic war set packaged to fit the show. The box reminds you to watch the series on ABC and contains a detailed list of what came in the set.

PUZZLE	**Milton Bradley**	**1964**	**30**	**17**	**9**

Milton Bradley made these hundred-piece Junior Jigsaw Puzzles with great regularity in the mid-sixties. The artwork is nice, but they never seem to sell for more than $50.

HOGAN'S HEROES

September 1965 - July 1971

It's 1942. London. World War II is in full swing. The postman brings a telegram: Your husband's plane has been shot down over Nazi Germany. He's been taken to a prisoner of war camp. Don't worry. If he's going to Stalag 13, he's going to have a riotous good time. Hogan and his heroes were residents of Germany's most prestigious prison camp. No one has ever escaped from Stalag 13. After all, who'd want to? The so-called "prisoners" have all the comforts of home—a French chef, a staff barber, women, and a pipeline right into German headquarters.

Running the camp was that exemplary leader of men, Col. Wilhelm Klink, stereotypically played by actor Werner Klemperer. Klink is played as the world's dumbest Nazi, who has a habit of taking military advice from his prisoners. At his side was his faithful, loyal watchdog Sgt. Schultz, played by John Banner. Banner clearly steals the show with his warm happy demeanor and his famous "I know nothing" reply just before he spills the beans. Inside the barracks was Bob Crane as Col. Robert Hogan. Although Crane was billed as the star of the show, his performance was generally overshadowed by an excellent supporting cast of colorful, albeit broadly painted characters with a mishmash of accents. Cooking the meals was Frenchman Louis LeBeau, played by Robert Clary. Richard Dawson of *Family Feud* fame got his start as Peter Newkirk, the card-playing cockney. Larry Hovis played slow-on-the-uptake Lt. Carter. For most of the series' run, Ivan Dixon appeared as Corp. Kinchloe, resident radio man. His part was taken over by Kenneth Washington in the last season.

Most of the comedy in this series came from the clever ruses the crew used to "escape" sabotage and return without ever being missed. As a subplot, Hogan and his men are constantly battling the German hierarchy in an effort to keep Klink in command of the camp. There are several good episodes with truly villainous Nazis that aren't as easily fooled as the monocled captain. As predictable as it may sound, *Hogan's Heroes* has a nice bank of surprise twists and double crosses that keep you watching all the way to the end. The characters are likable all, and the dialogue, especially that given to Banner, is up there with the best. Finally, if you're a true fan of the series, gather together four of your friends, fire up the harmonies, and sing. Although it has no words, the *Hogan's Heroes* theme is a great tune to sing. Try it.

Hogan's Heroes Collectibles

		Mint	Ex	Good
COMICS	Dell	66-69	20	10	4

Nine issues were produced, with the first seven having those great Dell photo covers.

			Mint	Ex	Good
GAME, BOARD	**Transogram**	1966	50	27	15

The Hogan's Heroes Bluff Out Game featured a sketch of the cast with close-up shots of Hogan and Klink facing off in the center of the lid. The board represented Stalag 13, with the object being to be the first player to escape from the POW camp. Rather depressing, don't you think?

			Mint	Ex	Good
GUM CARDS	**Fleer**	1966	200	110	60

The oddest thing about this set is that it wasn't made by Topps or Donruss. The set features photos from the series with rather lengthy captions, such as #43: "Schultz, there's not a strand of barbed wire left in this camp and I'd like to know why?" The wrappers and box have a cute design that uses head shots of Hogan, Schultz and Klink with cartoon bodies and backgrounds. The entire set of sixty-six cards is pretty rare. As a result, the box and wrapper will run you several hundred dollars each.

			Mint	Ex	Good
LUNCH BOX	**Aladdin**	1966	125	70	40

This is another rare domed metal box by Elmer Lenhardt. The artwork is very nice with good depth and color, although some of the likenesses are marginal. The box is designed to look like barracks with some of the characters looking out the windows while Hogan beguiles Schultz. The thermos shows Hogan preparing for a shave and a haircut.

			Mint	Ex	Good
MODEL	**MPC**	**1968**	**50**	**27**	**15**

This jeep model was little more than a generic jeep with a decal of Hogan's name on the side. The box is barely a step up, with three small photos of Klink, Schultz, and Hogan sporting his usual smirk.

		Mint	Ex	Good
RECORD	**Liberty Records**	**30**	**17**	**9**

"Hogan's Heroes Sing the Best of World War II" was produced as a premium. Though it is not a toy, it is a collectible that is not to be missed. Four actors, Dawson, Clary, Dickson and Hovis, act like singers, with tunes including "The Hogan's Heroes March."

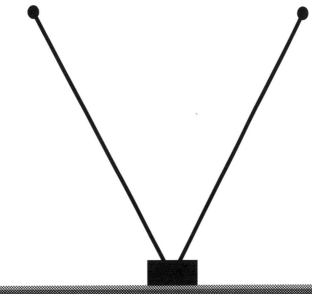

APPENDICES

TRIVIAL TELEVISION

Look for the answers in the sections related to each of the following TV shows.

What does U.N.C.L.E. stand for?

Name the ship the Robinsons were riding in when they were *Lost in Space*.

Name *Dark Shadows*' resident vampire.

It is rumored that a famous murderer auditioned to be a Monkee. Who was he?

Name the submarine that took us on a *Voyage to the Bottom of the Sea*.

What was the name of Buffy's doll on *Family Affair*?

How was Jed Clampett related to Elly May on *The Beverly Hillbillies*?

Sigfried worked for what evil organization on *Get Smart*?

What was the name of Bruce Wayne's elderly aunt on *Batman*?

What was Zorro's real identity?

What was the name of the Green Hornet's sidekick?

What actor played Daniel Boone?

What was the name of the Green Hornet's car?

Name the two children on *The Addams Family*.

Who was Ben Casey's mentor?

Which cast member lent his hand for the role of Thing in *The Addams Family*?

The Rat Patrol took place during World War II, but on what continent?

What was Darrin's occupation on *Bewitched*?

Name the villainous alien race that frequently visited the Enterprise on *Star Trek*.

What kind of gun did the Rifleman use?

Name all three children on *Family Affair*.	Whose Grandpa was "Grandpa" on *The Munsters*?	Who ran the town saloon in *Gunsmoke*?	Name all four Monkees. Take an extra point for their last names.	

Who was Napoleon's partner on *The Man from U.N.C.L.E.*?	Who uttered those infamous words "I know nothing!" on *Hogan's Heroes*?

Name the banker who cares for the Beverly Hillbillies.

Name the tiny balls of fur that gave the *Star Trek* crew "trouble."

Combat took place in World War II, but on what continent?

Name Lucas's son on *The Rifleman*.

What now famous movie actor played Dr. Kildare?

Name Samatha and Darrin's first baby on *Bewitched*.

Who was the original Riddler on *Batman*?

What was the Bloop on *Lost in Space*?

How many wives did Ben Cartwright have on *Bonanza*?

Name the evil organization that opposes U.N.C.L.E.

Name the ranch on *Bonanza*.

Name the Addams Family's hairy little relative.

What happened to General Savage on *Twelve O'Clock High*?

What phrases opened the credits of *The Outer Limits* every week?

BONUS BUCKS

Name the "witch" doctor on *Bewitched*.

What famous voice played the raven on *The Munsters*?

Where was the Spindrift going when it crashed on *The Land of the Giants*?

The Rat Patrol could be recognized by their four distinctive hats. What were they?

Give yourself two points for every right answer, five points for every bonus question. Add them up and see how you did.

0-15: You're obviously one of those healthy types who would prefer to jog instead of watch TV.

16-50: You're getting there. Crack open a copy of *TV Guide* and check back in a few weeks.

51-79: You're probably on your way to a *Star Trek* convention. Thanks for stopping by.

80-100: If you're not the chairman of Nick at Nite, you should be.

COLLECTING ON-LINE

Now you can talk about TV on another kind of screen, the one attached to your PC. On-line Bulletin Boards and World Wide Web sites have become the place to chat, exchange ideas, and find information. All of the major on-line services like America Online and CompuServe have TV forums and collecting forums. If you're an accomplished WEB walker, you can literally contact the world. Try some of these sites when looking for people who share the TV bug. Oh, by the way, while you're poking around cyberspace, drop me a line at CynthiaLil@aol.com.

America Online

Keyword: TV Gossip: In here you will find bulletin boards and a horde of archives containing such things as episode guides for *The Green Hornet* and a *Get Smart* gossip board. Look under syndicated and cable alphabetical listings for almost any show made in the sixties. If you don't find a board ready-made, start your own and see who joins you.

Keyword: Nick at Nite: Nick at Nite has their own site on AOL. The screen resembles a sixties TV and you can use the knobs to visit the rooms in the Nick at Nite house. Look for special offers and contests along with archives containing photos and sound clips from shows such as *Bewitched* and *The Munsters*.

World Wide Web

Http://ai.eecs.umich.edu/people/kennyp/sounds.html: This bit of gibberish will lead you to the TV Theme Song Home Page. The songs take forever to download unless you have an extremely fast modem, but once you get them the quality is great.

Http://scifi.com: This address will take you into the Sci-Fi Channel's home base, called The Dominion. Here you can swap stories about *Lost in Space*, *Land of the Giants* and other sci-fi/fantasy series of the sixties.

Internet

Use your Internet search mode to find the Rec.arts. section. There you will find news groups devoted to your old favorite shows, as well as groups on collecting toys, comics and gum cards.

Also check out your own on-line service in the entertainment area. Prodigy, CompuServe, and Delphi all have areas devoted to that other box in your living room.

SOURCES AND SUGGESTED READINGS

The Fifties and Sixties Lunch Boxes by Scott Bruce
Chronicle Books, 1988

Overstreet's Comic Price Guide
Updated yearly

The Addams Family Chronicle by Stephen Cox
Harper/Perenniel, 1991

The Monkees Tale by Eric Lefcowitz
Last Gasp, 1985

The Munsters by Stephen Cox
Contemporary Books, 1989

Hake's Guide to TV Collectibles by Ted Hake
Wallace-Homestead, 1990

Toys of the Sixties by Bill Bruegman
Cap'n Penny Productions, 1991

Spin Again by Rick Polizzi and Fred Schaefer
Chronicle Books, 1991

Prime Time Prime Movers by David Marc and Robert Thompson
Little, Brown and Company, 1992

The Complete Directory to Prime Time TV Stars by Tim Brooks
Ballantine, 1987

Cult TV by John Javna
St. Martin's Press, 1985

Toy Shop
Krause Publications (published bi-weekly)

DEALERS AND CLUBS

Toy Dealers

(The author would like to thank the following toy dealers for their help in making this book.)

General Toys and Memorabilia

Collectible Toys by Ann and Judy
PO Box 329
Sun City, CA 92586-0329
909-672-9502

Cartoon World
Steve Zoffreo
213-878-0611

Time Tunnel Toys
473 Bascom Ave.
San Jose, CA 95128
408-298-1709

Star Force Collectibles
Dwaine Williams
12922 Harbor Blvd.
Garden Grove, CA 92643
714-539-9525

Toy Seductions
Rob Chatlin
310-471-1040

Toyrific Toy Shows
Mike Stannard
PO Box 2037
San Bernardino, CA 92406
909-880-8558

Brad Leff
2118 Wilshire Blvd. #688
Santa Monica, CA 90403
818-710-9002

J & K Comics and Toys
PO Box 4014
Redondo Beach, CA 90278
310-542-4455

Toys from the Attic
20165 N. 67th Ave., Suite 122A
Glendale, AZ 85308
602-978-0925

Aurora Models

Ken Hunt
11590 Bari Dr.
Rancho Cucamonga, CA 91730
909-941-6402

Lunch Boxes

Luis Elliott
1840 S. Gaffey St. #16
San Pedro, CA 90731
310-832-4448

Joanna Privitera
345 F. Jeremiah Dr.
Simi Valley, CA 93065

In addition, thanks to:

Desi Scarpone, The Board Game Man

Renie Murphy of Murphy's Attic
David and Alisa Wolf
Jeff Berman, The Script Doctor
Glenn Holcomb

Fan Clubs

(The author does not guarantee the reliability of any of these clubs. Please inquire with a SASE.)

Addams Family/Munsters Club
Louis Wendruck
PO Box 69A04
West Hollywood, CA 90069

Batman
14755 Ventura Blvd.
Suite 1637
Sherman Oaks, CA 91403

Dark Shadows Fan Club
P.O. Box 92
Maplewood, NJ 07040

Irwin Allen Fan Club
11 Kimbolton Ct.
Kimbolton Rd.
Bedford, England MK40 2PH

Lost in Space
Flint Mitchell
7331 Terri Robyn
St. Louis, MO 63129
Producer of LISFAN magazine as well as books and memorabilia

Monkee Business Fanzine
c/o Maggie McManus
2770 South Broad St.
Trenton, NJ 08610

The Rat Patrol Dispatch
PO Box 28738
Santa Ana, CA 92799-8738

* For a listing of *Star Trek* fan clubs and others, check out the fan network in each issue of *Starlog* magazine.

About the Author

The author, Cynthia Boris Liljeblad (right), with her sisters, Linda (middle) and Chris (left), happily posing with their Christmas gifts--all '60s Mattel talking dolls: Sister Belle (left), Mattie Mattel (middle), and Casper (right).

Cynthia Boris Liljeblad has spent most of her adult life reacquiring all the toys she collected as a child. Writing professionally for the past six years, her articles have appeared in *Toy Collector, Collecting Toys, Epilogue Magazine* and *Toy Shop*. She currently writes a column on science fiction toys in *Toy Shop*. She is also co-author of *The Giants Are Coming* based on the *Land of the Giants* TV series.